THE
STUDIO

MÉMOIRE
DE LA VILLE
nrf

THE WORLD OF
ATELIER VIME

FRONT PORTFOLIO CAPTIONS

I. The courtyard of the Hôtel Drujon in Vallabrègues, with its elliptical arches, known as "basket arches" in French, which are reminiscent of the hôtels particuliers on Place aux Herbes in Uzès.
II. The entrance hall at Maison Vime in Vallabrègues.
III. An early nineteenth-century urn from Provence.
IV. The notebook designed by Wayne Pate, surrounded by a Medici trivet, an antique basket from Atelier Vime's archives, and a sixteenth-century Italian pelmet.
V. Alma in the summer living room at the house in Vallabrègues.
VI. The courtyard at Maison Vime in Vallabrègues.

FRENCH EDITION

Editorial Director: *Julie Rouart*
Administration Manager: *Delphine Montagne*
Editorial Manager: *Mélanie Puchault*,
assisted by *Adèle Ehlinger*
Design and Typesetting: *Marie-Lou Étienne*
Picture Research: *Lucía Pasalodos*

ENGLISH EDITION

Editorial Director: *Kate Mascaro*
Editor: *Helen Adedotun*
Translation from the French: *Bethany Wright*
Copyediting: *Lindsay Porter*
Proofreading: *Sarah Kane*
Production: *Élodie Conjat*
Color Separation: *Hyphen, Bergamo, Italy*
Printed in *Spain by Indice*

This book is typeset in Cardillac, Baskerville, and Hanken Grotesk, and is printed on Magno Volume 150 g.

Simultaneously published in French as
Atelier Vime: Histoire, lieux et formes

82 Rue Saint-Lazare
75009 Paris

editions.flammarion.com
@flammarioninternational

24 25 26 3 2 1

ISBN: 978-2-08-044562-9

Legal Deposit: 10/2024

THE WORLD OF

ATELIER VIME

A RENAISSANCE OF WICKER AND STYLE

Marie Godfrain
Benoît Rauzy
Anthony Watson

Flammarion

CONTENTS

Anthony Watson's family home in Avignon, featuring a monastery table set with Moustiers crockery, with painted eighteenth-century panels in the background.

WEAVING NATURE

Benoît Rauzy

The year is 2015. Emmanuel, the plasterer, is working on the molding on the staircase. Élise, the natural paint specialist, is applying a coat of colored casein whitewash using a brush; it fills the house with a strange curdled-milk smell that always reminds me of *kurut*—the little balls of dried sour milk sold in the markets of Central Asia.

For a year now, the Hôtel Drujon has been slowly coming back to life. Tons of terrazzo, cement, and paving have been removed and windows that had been walled up have been reopened, allowing light to pour in and bathe the stone floors and weathered walls. I am half-listening to the story Emmanuel is telling. When he was a child, he decided to dress up as a knight for Carnival, but he was missing the most important thing: a noble steed. So his father went down to the riverbank, cut some reeds, and used them to fashion him a horse. I am deeply moved by this story.

I've read Claude Lévi-Strauss's writings on basketwork; I've seen ancient statues holding woven baskets, with floor mosaics that pick up the pattern; I'm familiar with the delicate wicker baskets in the paintings of Antoine Raspal—an artist from Arles who painted scenes of daily life. But the point of Emmanuel's story is not about social science or art history; it doesn't evoke a remote land or a distant past. Instead, it illustrates the incredible power—the infinite privilege—of being able to give a child something they want, using nothing more than your own hands and a few reeds growing along the banks of a river.

We might say that Atelier Vime was born on that day, in this big house surrounded by scaffolding, which we expected to use merely as a vacation home. We were not exactly strangers to the village. Anthony, whose mother is from Provence, spent his childhood in an old château on a hill overlooking a village in the Gard region. As a young man, he was intrigued by an isolated village that spread along the riverbanks, which he saw while traveling along the road to Uzès. That was how, at the age of twenty-two, he came to buy a small house in Vallabrègues, which we renovated ourselves. We learned that three Roman roads—the Via Domitia, Via Aurelia, and Via Agrippa—met just a few miles away from the village, at the Chapel of Saint Gabriel in Tarascon—a symbolic meeting place for the ancient Iberian, Roman, and Gallic worlds. We knew about Beaucaire's magnificent houses, about its famous fair—the pride of the Sun King, Louis XIV—which brought prosperity to the region. We were familiar with the beautiful face of Anthony Vallabrègues, painted by Cézanne. He was descended from the "Pope's Jews," who, in the fifteenth century, had been sheltered by the village, which was at the southeastern tip of the papal enclave Comtat Venaissin, and had taken its name.

This maelstrom of empires and kingdoms, men and merchandise played a vital role in creating the incredible riches of this region between Languedoc and Provence. The wicker horse was like a compass pointing us toward a long and intimate history that we had not yet truly understood, that of the village that had been flooded a thousand times, the basins for soaking reeds in our courtyard, the shade of plane trees and acacias, the unbroken years of work by those who lived along the riverbanks.

The history was there. The house had even once been the site of a wickerwork business: Maison Boyer. If we couldn't continue this history—it was not ours to continue—we could at least revive the traditions and skills that we felt so connected to, across time and space.

One year later, Raphaelle Hanley joined us, with her signature sky-high heels and voluminous skirts. Together, we made our selections from her designs, which had the unified feel of an haute couture collection. Atelier Vime was born. We started making prototypes and received

Anthony Watson carrying planters in front of the willow field in Brittany.

the first mock-ups; then we had to find people to make them, and the craftspeople we had recruited in Provence could not manage it alone. So we went on the road. It was April but it was still snowing in the foothills of the Langres Plateau. The École Nationale d'Osiériculture et de Vannerie (National School of Reed-Growing and Basketry), at the heart of the town of Fayl-Billot, reminded me of a reform school. Affiliated with the French Ministry of Agriculture, this training center doesn't teach design, but agronomy and practical basket-weaving skills. Bakeries and restaurants are the main customers for French basket-makers, but the domestic industry has struggled to survive in the face of fierce competition from Asia and North Africa. The school is traditionally a place that offers students a second chance, or sometimes it is something of a last resort.

We also discovered that France does not produce enough reeds. "*Vime*," or osier willow, a plant used by basket-makers, has long been endemic to the region. Along with hedgerows, riverbanks and wetlands were the first victims of land consolidation and the drive to "develop" land that had not traditionally been cultivated. Wild reeds all but disappeared from the banks of rivers that had been canalized, and from Camargue, a region that was especially well suited to growing them. Therefore it was basket-makers who cultivated reedbeds, often relying heavily on pesticides. But as they were facing such stiff competition, craftspeople making baskets for practical uses had to work long hours to make a living and did not have time to grow their own reeds.

Plastic is not the only culprit responsible for the near decline of the French wickerwork industry. The craft is not highly valued; it is seen as quaint and old-fashioned, and there has been a significant drop in the number of people taking up professions in the sector. There were fifteen thousand basket-makers working in the 1950s, while today there are only around a hundred; many of them do not have access to networks of designers or sales outlets, which results in them being cut off from the business world. These figures represent a tragic loss of skills, culture, and diversity.

Our original, pioneering designs have shaken up an industry that is mainly focused on creating baskets for practical uses, and they often push craftspeople to the limits of their expertise. To realize them, we have to create molds and frameworks. We have to adapt weaving techniques so that they are capable of creating the innovative shapes of our designs. A single piece often takes more than forty hours of work.

Daybed from the 1960s, reupholstered in Décors Barbares fabric, with Les Olivades cushions.

We want to create beautiful objects; for us, the cost and challenges of producing them are secondary. When we set up our studio, we did none of the things that a business school would recommend: we didn't make a business plan, or conduct any market research. Instead, we rooted our project in the historic soil of Provence and tried, as best we could, to grow something that we found beautiful.

People were intrigued about the three of us and they liked our designs. Soon, we began to receive our first orders from prestigious names, especially in the United States. In May 2017, *Architectural Digest* published a profile on us, in which it described Atelier Vime as "the industry secret for designers." Is the New World really more open to new ideas, or is it that France is suspicious of them? We were, however, surprised by how elite our European clients were. Karl Lagerfeld was one of the first to buy the Medici vase, which would go on to become one of our brand's emblematic designs. To weave this piece, which stands over five feet two inches (160 cm) tall when placed on its pedestal, we use two wooden molds, one of which is placed inside the vase to keep it stable. It was Anthony who, while exploring the Maison Boyer archives, came across a design for a flower basket that the studio had produced in the 1940s—and decided to reimagine it.

We did not achieve this success on our own. I may have spoken of the sorry state of the wickerwork industry in France, but it is now time to praise its wonderful potential, its rigorous teaching methods, the impressive skills of master basket-makers, and the excellence of many craftspeople. Basket-makers traditionally work for themselves. When reading Charles Galtier's book *Entre Provence et Languedoc: Les Vanniers de Vallabrègues* (Between Provence and Languedoc: The basket-makers of Vallabrègues), I was surprised to discover that, in Vallabrègues, the price of baskets was fixed for the year and craftspeople were paid per item. In the late nineteenth century, changes to economic structures had led to the emergence of a new figure: the *patron vannier*, or head basket-maker, who handled all orders centrally and oversaw production. However, this did not lead to basket-makers receiving regular salaries or to commercial negotiations between the *patron* and individual craftspeople, which was by definition unequal. Although weavers worked for a *patron vannier*, they were free to look for work elsewhere, including with a different *patron*, if they needed money. This system also allowed craftspeople to choose what they would make, so that it suited their style. Our predecessors at Maison Boyer organized their business in this way, and it is still largely our approach today.

In 2020, the *Financial Times* named Atelier Vime one of "The World's Best Antique and Vintage Furniture Stores." From the very beginning, we had wanted to propose antique pieces alongside our new designs. Everything moved very quickly. Some of our favorite designers, whose work we had revived and promoted, experienced an explosion in popularity. That was the case for Adrien Audoux and Frida Minnet. Their collections of rope and rattan furniture, which was sold in their boutique in Juan-les-Pins, embodied the new "spirit of the Riviera." For thirty years or so, the Audoux-Minnet brand was emblematic of a sun-kissed way of life, which saw furniture that was designed to be used outdoors brought into the home, and its designs could be found from the Prince's Palace of Monaco to the porches of retirees on the Côte d'Azur.

We have been collectors for many years. Wicker, rattan, straw, and rope are materials that all the great designers of the twentieth century—from Charlotte Perriand to Paavo Tynell, and from Gio Ponti to André Arbus—used, celebrated, and even imitated: Jacques Adnet's bamboo is sometimes made of leather, Jean Després's rope is often in silver. Why? I don't know. But it was by combining these pieces with classic French antiques, which many people considered old-fashioned, that Atelier Vime's style was born. Anthony and I have always lived our lives surrounded by antiques. They are like our mother tongue, the language in which we can best choose our words and form our own sentences.

Without any formal training, we learned as we went along, and our house's "personality" grew stronger. The Hôtel Drujon in Vallabrègues is a wonderful setting for interior design. There is something very touching about the architecture, which is refined and elegant but still remains functional, close to daily life, with no hint of pretentiousness. We were careful to preserve the poetry of the main buildings. It was a different story when it came to the outbuildings (which we bought when they fell vacant), as these had undergone extensive "modernization" in the 1950s and 1970s.

Today, visitors to Maison Vime step inside buildings that we have completely renovated using traditional materials and natural paint. We commissioned paving made with pebbles from the riverbed, which was traditionally used in the courtyards of houses in the village. Embedded in mortar mixed with whitewash, the pebbles allow water to run off without artificializing the soil, therefore allowing it to breathe. Another advantage of this type of paving is that it does not store heat in the summer. Despite the material's beneficial properties, the mayor told us that we were the first people in the village to use this technique for more than a century.

The effects of climate change can be clearly felt in Provence, especially in Camargue. The climate there is becoming less and less suited to growing reeds. We have therefore decided to grow our raw materials in Brittany, where we have family land, and we do so without using any pesticides. As well as the varieties of reed that we use for our own creations, the land also has a field of lavender and immortelle (dwarf everlast), and an old orchard of apple and pear trees. Overlooking a sound, which swells and empties to the rhythm of the tides, the reedbed is a beautiful island of biodiversity—a constant source of joy and inspiration.

The interior design industry's environmental impact is considerable: products of mediocre quality use astronomical quantities of raw materials, often grown in terrible conditions; fast-growing tree species use vast amounts of water and increase the likelihood of fires. Intentionally creating products with a short lifespan is even more disgraceful when they are targeted at consumers who are increasingly concerned about the environment and are making an ethical choice to buy products made from natural materials.

These are important considerations for us. We are a luxury brand, but this luxury begins at the heart of our reedbed, at the point where land meets sea in Finistère.

In a modest wooden frame, facing the desk in my bedroom on the Brittany farm, an elegant man wearing traditional Breton costume crosses what looks like the Place Saint-Corentin in Quimper. His black eyes and olive skin are at odds with his attire and surroundings. And with good reason, because the man whom Max Jacob painted in gouache for his book *The Coast: A Collection of Celtic Songs* (1926) is his grandfather, Samuel Alexandre, a tailor by profession. Originally from the Rhineland, he moved to Quimper, and less than ten years later his traditional Breton costumes won him the silver medal at the Paris Exposition Universelle in 1867. Like the tailor of those "Celtic songs," we are not quite Provençal nor entirely Breton. Our strong, deeply-rooted identity owes as much to the skies and the walls of our childhood, which have left their mark on us, as to our quests as adults and the places where our choices lead us.

In April 2023, we began a new project, following the purchase of a large property in Normandy, surrounded by fertile land. The château is a "house of the fields"—one of those country retreats built in the eighteenth century by bourgeois or aristocratic families. It is not yet time to reveal the nature of this project, but it seems important to me, in the concluding lines of this book's introduction, to say that our story is still being written.

FACING PAGE
A harmonious encounter between an encoignure and a daybed attributed to Louis Sognot.

PAGES 12–13
View of the village of Baux-de-Provence.

AN INTRODUCTION TO WICKER

WICKERWORK THROUGHOUT HISTORY

Plant matter has been woven since time immemorial, and the practice dates back to the very beginnings of human history. Very early on, people found ways of using leaves, stalks, and grasses to create objects that allowed them to trap animals or transport goods. Wickerwork is an ancient skill, so commonplace and so deeply rooted in daily life that very few written traces of it survive today. However, it was one of the most common—and essential—practices used by various cultures around the world, up until the Industrial Revolution. From the dawn of civilization, wickerwork made transport easier by allowing people to create containers in various shapes that were both lightweight and durable, and could be immersed in water. Different methods were needed, depending on what the baskets were designed to hold and how they were intended to be carried by humans or animals, and weaving techniques thus gradually developed over time.

Although it is difficult to give a precise date for the advent of wickerwork, it is believed to be one of the oldest crafts in the world. Archeologists have not been able to find many physical traces of the technique because the plant fibers used in weaving are perishable. Baskets disintegrate, the bottoms come off and rot. Fortunately, there are numerous depictions of wickerwork in the frescoes and paintings of early civilizations, as well as imprints left on Neolithic pottery (see below). During this period, wickerwork was used to make molds: the bottoms of baskets were coated with clay, which dried to form dishes. Some indigenous groups in North America still use this technique today, using coiled baskets to make pottery.

It was during the Neolithic era—in the Stone Age and Bronze Age more precisely—that wickerwork is believed to have been invented. The oldest known pieces of wickerwork were discovered in the Fayoum region in Upper Egypt. They date back more than ten thousand years. Historians believe that wickerwork may have played a role in the development of agriculture, especially cultivating crops with small seeds, as baskets allowed people to store and transport them easily. As researchers Hélène Balfet and Jacques Anquetil explained in their 1979 book *La Vannerie* (Basketry), "For at least seven thousand years, making mats, baskets, and traps was almost universal. The only way to understand the centrality of wickerwork in the Neolithic era, in material, religious, and social terms, is by studying certain tribes that still remain primitive today."[1]

Over time, each civilization developed the craft according to its own needs and the resources it had available, as well as its level of technological advancement. The Mesopotamian civilization predominantly used reeds: when coated with pitch, they became watertight and rotproof. According to a legend that recalls the biblical tale of Moses in the Old Testament, when King Sargon of Akkad was a baby, his mother placed him in a round basket and abandoned him on the waters of the Tigris River. At that time, along the Euphrates and the Tigris, people used small boats in the form of large baskets made of woven reeds that were covered in skins and coated with pitch. There are numerous examples depicted on Assyrian bas-reliefs. These kinds of skiffs are still used today by local populations living along the Tigris. Many objects were made of wicker, such as chairs, chests, baskets, shields, and chariots (see below), to name but a few.

BELOW, FROM LEFT TO RIGHT

Fragments of the base of a vase with woven imprint, fourth century BCE. Pottery, Musée d'Archéologie Nationale, Saint-Germain-en-Laye.

Relief depicting the chariot of King Ashurbanipal and Elamite prisoners, from the Palace of Ashurbanipal in Nineveh, c. 645 BCE. Gypsum alabaster, Musée du Louvre, Paris.

Scenes of sowing and harvesting, Tomb of Ounsou, discovered at Thebes, eighteenth dynasty (c. 1550–1292 BCE). Musée du Louvre, Paris.

FACING PAGE

Tile depicting fish escaping from a basket, second century. Mosaic, Sousse Archeological Museum, Sousse (Tunisia).

In Ancient Egypt, during the Neolithic era, baskets were made in the shape of boats (examples have been discovered in tombs), and most sarcophagi were woven from plant fibers. Here again, there are depictions in the form of bas-reliefs and statues that allow us to imagine woven objects, like the basket that appears in a fresco from the Middle Kingdom (see page 16, right) and similar examples found in the tomb of Rameses III.[2]

On the other side of the Mediterranean, the abundance of texts and visual depictions, as well as artifacts discovered through archeological excavations of sites buried by the eruption of Vesuvius, testify to the importance of wickerwork in the Roman Empire, where it was used for diverse and varied objects, "whose usage was widespread throughout daily life."[3] People began to use a number of different plants, depending on the geographical and geological regions, to create implements in various forms. We find ample evidence in the profusion of terms used in Latin literature to refer to baskets: *qualum*, *sirpia*, *sporta*, *varro*, *scirpea*, *scirpiculus*, *calathus*, *aero*, *ero*, *hero*, *fiscus*, *vitile*, *vegetius*, *metella*, *canistrum*, *sportula*, *fiscina*. This variety can also be seen in many different artistic forms: sculptures (in which wicker is one of the few materials whose appearance can be accurately rendered), murals and mosaics (see pages 16 and 17, and above), figurines, and even crockery and other decorated objects.[4]

ABOVE
Basket of figs, first century. Fresco, Villa Poppaea, Oplontis (Italy).

FACING PAGE, LEFT
Ottoman Bread Seller, c. 1775. Watercolor, School of Oriental and African Studies Library, London.

FACING PAGE, RIGHT
A Baker, c. 1735. Colored etching, Musée des Arts Décoratifs, Paris.

And what about other parts of the world? North America has always been a leading country for the technique of weaving plant fibers. The oldest surviving baskets were discovered in caves in the arid regions of the southwestern United States, in Nevada and Utah. For Native Americans, wickerwork goes beyond the utilitarian function that we traditionally associate with it; the practice has much greater importance, as it is related to a number of religious traditions and baskets were used for bartering.

In Asia, bamboo is the main material used for weaving, especially in Japan, but it is in Borneo that we find some of the most varied and sophisticated wickerwork in Southeast Asia; the most predominant are ritual objects such as rattan mats with rich geometric or figurative motifs in two colors, but everyday items such as shallow conical hats or baby carriers can also be found.

In Africa, we come across similar objects, made using a greater variety of plant fibers, especially in the forested tropical regions; the latter are rich in foliage, palm leaves, and vines, which have been used by many groups since the earliest times to weave various everyday objects. In the savannah regions, millet, sorghum, and dwarf palm leaves are used to weave portable grain stores.

In Europe, willow was the preferred material for wickerwork, although craftspeople often used other wild plants that they gathered from woods or hedges. Osier, a species of willow, is the plant most often used in France, and the wickerwork industry gave rise to the practice of cultivating osier, which thrives in poor-quality, damp soil that is not well suited to growing other plants. Osier willow has very long, supple branches that can be used whole or split into splints, and can be kept in their natural state or used with their bark stripped off. Historians agree that the French term *vannier*, which means basket-maker, comes

from *van*, meaning a winnowing basket. These woven conch-shaped baskets with two handles appear in Egyptian mythology. Later, in the fifth century, winnowing baskets were used at Dionysian festivals to hold the first fruits of the grape harvest being offered to the gods.

In France, the guild of basket-makers was officially recognized in 1467, when it was issued with letters patent registered in parliament by Louis XI. The corporation was dissolved in 1776; at that time it was not considered to be representative of the diversity of the basket-making profession, which included domestic basket-makers, traveling basket-makers, artisanal basket-makers, and those who practiced the activity to supplement their income.[5] Later, in the eighteenth and nineteenth centuries, basket-makers generally belonged to apprenticeship networks: they went from town to town to hone their skills with the best craftspeople, and when their tour of France was finished, they created a masterpiece: an intricate and often enormous wickerwork statue. The patron saint of basket-makers is Saint Anthony the Great, who, according to legend, earned his living from weaving baskets. Saint Anthony's feast day is celebrated on January 17, during the cold season, when osier willow is harvested.

In the early nineteenth century, wickerwork flourished thanks to the rise of the middle classes, who provided a market for home comforts. Up until the end of the century, wicker objects were adapted to suit the needs of agriculture and local industries: along the coasts, basket-making

was focused on weaving containers for fishing and transporting fish and shellfish; in wine-growing regions, wicker was used to make protective packaging for bottles and baskets for carrying grapes. The craft flourished in a number of regions in France where the soil was well suited to growing osier willow (Aisne, Ain, along the Rhône, Charentes, Corrèze, Côte d'Or, Garonne, Meurthe-et-Moselle, Val-de-Loire, and Vendée). However, it also emerged in other disparate locations thanks to fortuitous circumstances: for example, in Fayl-Billot, in the Haute-Marne region, where a monk who was a skilled basket-maker moved three hundred and fifty years ago and passed on his skills, first to the other monks in his community, then to local residents.

Basket-makers also adapted their work to meet different needs at different times: they made eel traps, washing baskets, demijohns, baskets for carrying snails or strawberries (see facing page). The craft experienced an unprecedented surge with the arrival of the railway in the nineteenth century, which connected all of France. Perishable foodstuffs—fish, fruit, and delicate vegetables—had previously been luxury items because they were difficult to transport, but now they could be transported more quickly and in greater quantities; their prices dropped, which in turn led to greater demand for containers.

FACING PAGE
Jean-Baptiste Siméon Chardin, *Basket of Wild Strawberries*, c. 1761. Oil on canvas, Musée du Louvre, Paris.

ABOVE
Caravaggio, *Boy with a Basket of Fruit*, 1593–1594. Oil on canvas, Galleria Borghese, Rome.

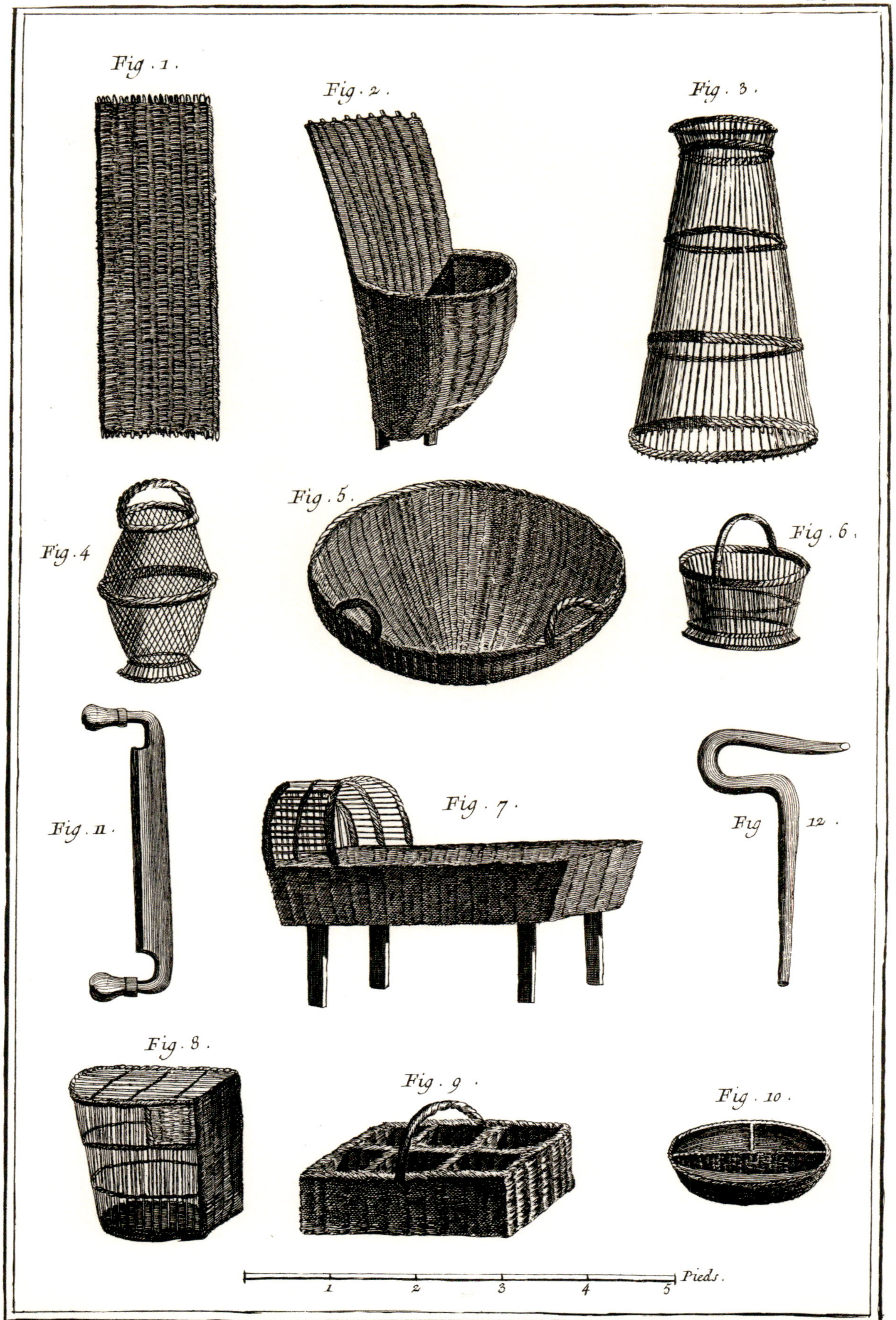

Bourgeois Del. Benard Fecit

Vannier, Ouvrages et Outils.

This was also the era of "The Ladies' Paradise": it witnessed the inauguration of department stores, as well as the emergence of a consumer society and of a middle class eager to accumulate objects that were desired rather than needed. This spurred a shift from the production of objects that were purely functional toward objects that symbolized a certain lifestyle—trinket bowls, travel trunks, birdcages, babies' rattles, little candy baskets, and a whole host of other knickknacks.

Workshops began to develop and thrive, until the introduction of plastic in the 1960s. Then, in the 1970s, the increased importation of objects and furniture from Asia took its toll on the livelihoods of artisan basket-makers. Although basket-making gradually disappeared from daily life in the twentieth century, the craft inspired designers, who created avant-garde pieces in wicker and rattan combined with metal—a material that was emblematic of modernity. These twentieth-century designers, from the most well-known names to the best-kept secrets, have always interested Anthony Watson and Benoît Rauzy, and this goes a long way to explain why Atelier Vime has become a reference for designer creations in natural materials.

Charlotte Perriand is one such renowned designer to have incorporated wickerwork into her designs. In the early days of her career she created metal furniture, but after World War II she started working with natural materials, as seen in her Rio coffee table, which is composed of six rattan segments of different radii, surrounded by an

FACING PAGE
Trade plate for the profession of basket-maker, from *Encyclopédie, ou Dictionnaire raisonné des sciences, des arts et des métiers* (Systematic dictionary of the sciences, arts, and crafts), eighteenth century. Private collection.

ABOVE
Antoine Raspal, *A Sewing Workshop in Arles*, 1760. Oil on canvas, Musée Réattu, Arles.

uneven wooden border. Louis Sognot, who began working with Perriand in the 1930s, decided to combine rattan with modern materials such as metal, as in the chair he designed with Charlotte Alix, which is made of burgundy-lacquered tubular metal with a woven rattan backrest and seat. At the Salon des Arts Ménagers in 1939, he presented a hotel room furnished entirely in rattan. After the war, he would come to be seen as the top designer of rattan furniture in France, and he was awarded first prize for rattan at the Salon des Artistes Décorateurs in 1952.

One of their contemporaries, the architect and interior designer Jacques Adnet, adopted a modernist style throughout the 1930s before embracing a more traditional, neoclassicist approach after World War II. His wicker designs included chairs with heart-shaped backrests, a drinks trolley made of topstitched leather and wicker, a coat rack and mirror made of wicker and metal, and a planter made of brass and wicker. He enjoyed using the material for a wide variety of everyday objects and furniture, as did his fellow designer Mathieu Matégot, who was famous for his perforated metal furniture, but also designed wicker furniture in simple shapes, including an armchair made from a wicker dome placed on a metal structure.

Janine Abraham and Dirk-Jan Rol drew on similar sources of inspiration to create designs with clean lines using unprocessed natural materials. From the late 1950s onward, Abraham & Rol created furniture for a number of apartments, as well as designing pieces that were released in 1957 by Rougier, the go-to rattan furniture company at the time. Their work was characterized by an economic use of materials, with a simplicity and clarity that are highly regarded today.

In the same period, Joseph-André Motte founded the Atelier de Recherche Plastique (ARP) with Pierre Guariche and Michel Mortier. Motte made his name in 1954 with the release of his Christera easy chair, which had three legs and was made entirely of woven rattan core, and his Catherine chair, which had a wide circular seat made from rattan core resting on a base with three slanted metal legs. Christera was also

ABOVE, FROM LEFT TO RIGHT

Christian Dior sitting in an Audoux-Minnet armchair, Lavandoux, 1955.

Rattan furniture by Louis Sognot, 1955. Photograph published in *Nouvel Art du logis*.

Christera easy chair in rattan, created by Joseph-André Motte, c. 1949, edited by Rougier, and presented at the Paris Salon in 1953.

FACING PAGE

Bedroom for an artistic young girl, shown at the Salon des Décorateurs in 1947. Sycamore furniture, with a painting of a bouquet of flowers by Madeleine Arbus and a portrait of Arbus by Marc Saint-Saens on the walls.

the name given to one of the most famous designs by Jacques Hitier, an interior designer who studied at the École Boulle in Paris. Hitier worked for fifteen years with the company Tubauto, designing a number of pieces of furniture which were mainly made from metal tubes combined with soft materials such as wood, fabric, or rattan. His iconic Christera armchair, released in 1950, boasts a backrest with daring ergonomic curves.

French reconstruction designer Roger Landault worked on a diverse range of projects, including luxury designs and reconstruction furniture, and he infused his designs encompassing canework and rattan core structures with this same openness. He knew how to make the most of these materials, which he combined with other, more elegant raw materials to create ergonomic designs that were anchored in daily life.

Finally, André Arbus—one of Atelier Vime's favorite designers—associated interior design in the classic French "grande décoration" style with a very modern treatment of natural materials.

And France was not the only country to succumb to the charms of rattan after World War II. In Italy, especially—the spiritual home of design—some of the most famous modern designers, including figures such as Franca Helg, Franco Albini, Gio Ponti, and Ico Parisi, also started to adopt wicker and rattan as their favored materials.

S. Gabriel
Maillane
Sillon
Le Fort d'herau
Lonsac
Tarascon
Beaucaire
Valabregues
117
118
119
114
115
116
Poste
Comps
chau de. St. Romans
jonquieres
St. Vincens
Etang de jonquieres

WICKER: A STORY OF WATER, ALONG THE BANKS OF THE RHÔNE

For millennia, the people of Vallabrègues—a village founded in 3500 BCE between Camargue and Languedoc—have grown osier willow and worked with wicker. Cut off from major transport routes, Vallabrègues's geography was shaped by the caprices of the Rhône, along whose banks it was built. The village was an island until the river's course changed in the mid-eighteenth century. Living on the water's edge naturally led the villagers to turn to osier willow cultivation and wickerwork. There is evidence of a corporation of *banastiers* (makers of *banastes*: small, usually handleless baskets) in the Arles region as early as the thirteenth century. "Sociologists and ethnologists have not paid much attention to this artisanal community. We know, vaguely, that in the village of Vallabrègues, 'somewhere along the banks of the Rhône,' there was a population of basket-makers," explains the academic Charles Galtier, author of a doctoral thesis that he defended in February 1968. This thesis was a landmark work on the subject of the basket-makers of Vallabrègues. It reveals that in 1911, the village had 320 basket-makers out of a total of 1,818 inhabitants, which represents 17 percent and the majority of the village's working population.

The symbiotic relationship between the village, with its narrow white limestone lanes, and the Rhône, which runs alongside it, is documented in a number of texts. As vital as it is destructive, the river has always been a fickle friend to the inhabitants of Vallabrègues, and even led to the introduction of specific laws that were created for the village. In his book *Entre Provence et Languedoc: Les Vanniers de Vallabrègues*, Charles Galtier explains this special connection: "The nature of the land around Vallabrègues, the fragility of its soil, the range of physical factors all make it a region that is better suited to people of the water, like basket-makers, than to farmers, who are people of the soil; for many years the only way to access the island of Vallabrègues was by water. Relations with the outside world relied on river transport on the Rhône, and the basket-makers had a flotilla of small boats.

Map of the Rhône River, from Vivarais to the sea (detail), eighteenth century.

The plantations of osier willow on the banks of the Rhône are called 'baisses,' and the basket-makers who worked with the resulting wicker were given the name 'baissiers.'"[6]

The village archives detail the long list of destructive floods and recount an endless series of stories in which villagers were cut off in their homes, unable to work to earn a living, forced to travel by boat, and suffered from hunger because the rising water had flooded their land. And yet, despite all of these hardships, they clung to this land, which was also life-giving.

The village of Vallabrègues has preserved an impressive number of old land registers, known as *compoix*, the oldest of which dates back to 1430. Keeping these records required a significant amount of work, which the authorities in France rarely undertook. But in Vallabrègues, the Rhône forced their hand. Over the years, the changes in the river's course meant that the available land shifted. These plots of land were subject to a special, very old local law: the *déguisements* of the Rhône. This law stipulated that "land that has been destroyed" should be replaced with "land that has been newly created": landowners were therefore compensated for the loss of terrains henceforth covered by the Rhône by receiving new ones that had appeared elsewhere. This obliged the community to regularly revise its land registry documents to take into account the new land that had been uncovered and the land that

ABOVE
Cane from Provence waiting to be split, with the workshop—today Maison Vime—in the background.

FACING PAGE
Sorting the cane—an everyday sight on the village's circular boulevard.

had been reclaimed by the river. The practice gave rise to a number of disputes, disagreements, and lawsuits, as is evident from the many rulings that appear in the village records.

For his *Histoire de Vallabrègues*,[7] Louis Popovitch immersed himself in the village archives, from the ancient Roman era up until the twentieth century. He writes that, in the eighteenth century, the Rhône changed course to the west of the village; the resulting reallocation of land sparked a mini revolution that was ahead of its time, and it led to the toppling of the consul of Vallabrègues. On April 5, 1712, the king issued a decree to calm the situation.

A number of famous authors have been inspired by the tumultuous relationship between the people of Vallabrègues and the Rhône. In Chapter 9 of *Bric-à-Brac*, a collection of memories, anecdotes, and stories published in 1836, Alexandre Dumas presents Jacques Fosse, a grain merchant from Beaucaire and lifeguard in his spare time, who recounts the floods that struck Vallabrègues in 1836, leaving the village entirely surrounded by water, with all communication cut off. He describes a completely flooded island, where all the villagers took refuge in the cemetery, since it was the highest point in the village and the only place that was not under water.

In his autobiography *Au pays de Vincent (mon métier de vannier)* (In the land of Vincent [my job as a basket-maker]),[8] José de Vallabrègues relates his childhood memories from the early twentieth century, growing up in a family of basket-makers:

> In addition to all the challenges of having a workshop outside of the home, there were also periods of flooding. And although they were not usually very serious, they were very frequent. As the Rhône often flooded the street without the water coming inside the workshop, there was no question of stopping work. We would not have been able to make a living if we had done so! But how could we travel between the house and the workshop when the road was covered in water? Well, quite simply, by using a neighbor's boat, as he was kind enough to lend it to us! My father tied it to the door of the workshop, and in the evening the whole family got in, often in the rain, and set off down the road to sleep in the small family home, which was not only freezing, as usual, but also much wetter because the ground floor was flooded.

In the twentieth century, a number of major works were undertaken to better manage the whims of the Rhône: a reinforced wharf was built and pumps were installed to channel sewers and rainwater into the river. But these changes were not enough. There were many floods throughout the winter of 1935–1936, and the waters reached a height of over six feet (two meters) in the village, which meant that farmers were unable to work, plunging them into poverty.

FACING PAGE
Women peeling osier willow on the islands of the Rhône, from an illustration by Jules Laurens. Plate published in *L'Illustration*, Paris, 1860.

ABOVE
Paul André Basset, *Beaucaire Fair and a View of Tarascon*, eighteenth century. Colored etching, Musée des Arts Décoratifs, Paris.

"The Rhône has always been the main concern of our population: an excellent means of transport, the impulsion behind the founding of Vallabrègues, nourishing, lethal, devastating—by turns God or Devil," writes Louis Popovitch.

There was another nearby town on the banks of the Rhône, which provided a significant market for the baskets produced in Vallabrègues: Beaucaire. Due to its location, it became an important trading port. In July 1464, the town hosted its first annual fair, the Fair of Saint Mary Magdalene, which soon became an essential meeting place for merchants from around the world. The town's location in the South of France, near to the port of Marseille, made it easy to transport merchandise there. Goods were sold on the boats themselves, in the fair—from stalls made of wood or canvas—and in the town, on the ground floor of many houses. They included all kinds of merchandise, from cloth or jewelry to crockery, furniture, or spices. The fair introduced people to new techniques and materials from abroad, such as indigo and floral *indienne* fabrics. After centuries of prosperity, which made the town famous—it was said that everything could be bought and sold at the Beaucaire Fair—the event slowly began to wane throughout the nineteenth century. However, traces of it still remain today: a grand parade, organized by the town, is held on the evening of July 21, allowing inhabitants to reconnect with their history.

Thanks to the arrival of the railway, Provence became a popular destination for artists, who were drawn there by the unique culture. Throughout the twentieth century, many painters and writers drew inspiration from the rich soil of this region. Among them were photographers who came to Vallabrègues to capture basket-makers at work in their rudimentary workshops scattered around the village. They came to document a world that was fast disappearing, due to the advent of plastic in the 1960s, which gradually began to replace wicker. Lucien Clergue was a thirty-four-year-old, little-known photographer from Arles when he traveled around the region, immortalizing its customs and culture in a series of portraits. He photographed Vallabrègues in 1966. Robert Doisneau, who was already a well-established photographer, was interested in documenting manual skills that had fallen out of fashion and traditional crafts at risk of becoming extinct. It is not known how he discovered Vallabrègues, but his portraits of its basket-makers are some of the most famous visual records of the village's history.

ABOVE
Robert Doisneau, *The Basket-Maker of Vallabrègues*, 1966.

FACING PAGE
Lucien Clergue, *Soaking Osier Willow in a Village* Ramieu, 1966.

ATELIER VIME: RECONNECTING WITH THE PAST

Among the basket-makers of Vallabrègues, the Boyer family played a major role in the history of the village, especially that of the Hôtel Drujon, which the founders of Atelier Vime purchased in 2014.

The story begins during the Restoration, after the fall of the First Empire in 1815, when Étienne Dominique Drujon, a potter from the neighboring village of Meynes, married Marthe Apollonie Gabriellot, a young woman from a family of basket-makers in Vallabrègues. The couple moved into this elegant house, which had been built around 1730, during the reign of Louis XV. Over the course of several generations, the Drujon family rose through the ranks of society. In 1850, Adolphe Drujon, who trained at the Bar, moved to Tarascon; the young lawyer went into local politics, becoming mayor of the town and president of the departmental council. It was also in 1850 that the Falloux law obliged local councils to provide elementary schooling for girls. School was not mandatory, and it was not free; the house that Adolphe had vacated was turned into an elementary school with a classroom for local middle-class girls, as well as accommodation for three nuns, who worked as teachers. In the 1870s, education became free, secular, and obligatory—one of the ambitious projects of the Third Republic—and the town had to find another site that could better accommodate the large numbers of students. In a happy coincidence, the merchant Armand Boyer bought the house in 1878 for the sum of 6,000 francs and moved his basket-making workshop there; it was continued by his descendants until the late 1970s. The workshop was given a final lease of life when Aramis Boyer, who had retired from the SNCF, the French national rail company, returned to live and weave baskets in Vallabrègues; the activity died out with him in 1982.

Anthony Watson and Benoît Rauzy, the founders of Atelier Vime.

The Hôtel Drujon is not an intimidating building, despite its spacious size. On the ground floor, a series of arches allows light to penetrate all the way to the back of the building, while keeping the air cool. The central staircase does not have a window on the first two floors, but, 25 feet (8 meters) above the ground, a row of five windows face due west. As well as letting in light, they provide a beautiful view of the colors of the setting sun. This row of windows, which can be seen from the far bank of the Rhône, embraces the principle of *montrance* that is typical of Provençal architecture—a kind of "showing off" that was central to mid-eighteenth-century customs, which placed great importance on distinguishing between the public and private spheres. In the courtyard were constructed three *ramieus*—stone basins used for soaking willow—which would have allowed the fifteen or so basket-makers to work in the heart of the house.

Shortly after Benoît Rauzy and his partner Anthony Watson bought the house in Vallabrègues in 2014, Benoît came across a book, which plunged him into the world of wicker. Or, more precisely, a doctoral thesis: "Vallabrègues: Un village de vanniers," submitted by Charles Galtier to the University of Montpellier in 1968. Rauzy devoured this work, which described an ecosystem that was dying out. The study explored the forms of apprenticeship, the ways in which technical skills were passed on, and the evolution of social structures that, for centuries, allowed a community to make a living from one trade: basket-making.

At the same time, Anthony Watson was learning about the history of their home, situated on a narrow lane at the center of the village. He discovered that the eighteenth-century building had belonged to

BELOW
Basket-makers from Fayl-Billot and their creations, early twentieth century.

FACING PAGE
Letterhead of producer-merchant basket-maker Camille Boyer, Atelier Vime archives.

MANUFACTURE DE VANNERIE EN TOUS GENRES

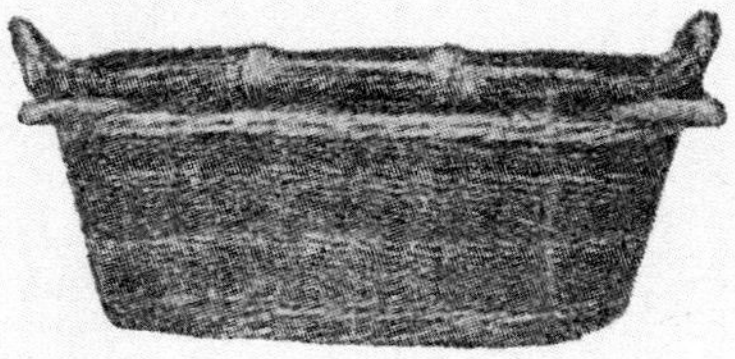

GRISE & BLANCHE

BANASTES, BILLOTS

Paniers à Choux-Fleurs

SPÉCIALITÉ
DE
Grandes MANNES en CANNES

MANNES & PANIERS CARRÉS
pour Négociants en Fruits et Primeurs

Adresse Télégraphique et Postale :
CAMILLE BOYER, VALLABRÈGUES

R. C. NIMES N° 1770

Camille Boyer
PROPRIÉTAIRE-NÉGOCIANT
à **VALLABRÈGUES** (Gard)

Le 11 Mars 1931

Monsieur L. Bonnefond et Cie
Ampuis.

En réponse à votre honoré du 10 courant, je pourrais vous fournir des mannes en canne et couverts bombés.

Je fournis ces emballages à beaucoup d'expéditeurs de Tarascon et de la région, pour l'expédition des épinards.

Je vous fournirai des 16/16 pouces sans anses, avec couverts au prix de 8,50 ; ou des 18/18 et couverts à 10 f. l'un, paniers marqués L B au goudron noir, en bas sous la torche ; au besoin je vous enverrai échantillon.

Si ces grandeurs faisaient votre affaire, je suis à votre disposition.

Je vous assure une bonne marchandise.

Entre temps d'être favorisé de vos ordres.

Recevez Monsieur mes salutations empressées

C. Boyer

Mes lettres ne m'engagent que pour un courrier.
Mes marchandises sont vendues sur gare départ et voyagent aux risques et périls du destinataire.
Mes marchandises sont payables dans Vallabrègues sans dérogation.

a family of basket-makers and was home to one of the most important basket-making workshops in the village. This find inspired in the two men a new passion for the craft. They decided to establish Atelier Vime and, with the designer Raphaelle Hanley, they put together their first sketches of hanging baskets, mirrors, screens, and pillars, among other items.

But why "Atelier Vime?" In Latin, *Salix viminalis* refers to a kind of willow that is particularly supple and durable. The French word *vime* is derived from it, and refers to the osier willow used by basket-makers.

Anthony Watson and Benoît Rauzy traveled around the region in search of basket-makers—a nearly defunct profession, although the village still holds a European festival of basket-making every summer. "Here, wicker is a cultural, historical matter. Everything was right there, within arm's reach," explains Anthony Watson. "But everything had to be restarted from scratch and rebuilt." They met Béatrice, a wicker-worker, and Pamela, a straw and cane specialist. They were interested in the project and agreed to weave the full-scale models sketched by Raphaelle Hanley on large sheets of paper taped together, like huge maps that revealed the enormity of the task to be accomplished. Thanks to them, Atelier Vime was born! Success was waiting just around the corner. Their creations have been featured in some of the most beautiful interiors all around the globe.

"There were many who predicted that we would move production abroad, but our approach is exactly the opposite: we want to anchor it in the land," explains Anthony Watson. Thanks to its growth, Atelier Vime has become a key player in French artisanal basket-making, but the basket-makers of Beaucaire have continued to create the prototypes and are committed to training craftspeople locally. And so the story continues, a stone's throw from the river, in this courtyard where, in the past, fifteen basket-makers worked around the *ramieus*, in which they dipped branches of osier willow to soften them before they began weaving.

Anaëlle Audibert runs Maison Vime. Passionate about art and craftsmanship, she grew up in the village.

NOTES

1 Hélène Balfet and Jacques Anquetil, *La Vannerie* (Paris: Dessain et Tolra, 1979).
2 Ibid.
3 Magali Cullin-Mingaud, *La Vannerie dans l'Antiquité romaine* (Paris: CNRS, Collection du Centre Jean Bérard, 2010).
4 Ibid.
5 Martine Jaoul and Bernadette Goldstein, *La Vannerie française* (Paris: Musée National des Arts et Traditions Populaires/RMN, 1990).
6 Charles Galtier, *Entre Provence et Languedoc: Les Vanniers de Vallabrègues* (Grenoble: Centre Alpin et Rhodanien d'Ethnologie, 1980).
7 Self-published.
8 José de Vallabrègues, *Au pays de Vincent (mon métier de vannier)* (Nîmes: Camariguo, 1983).

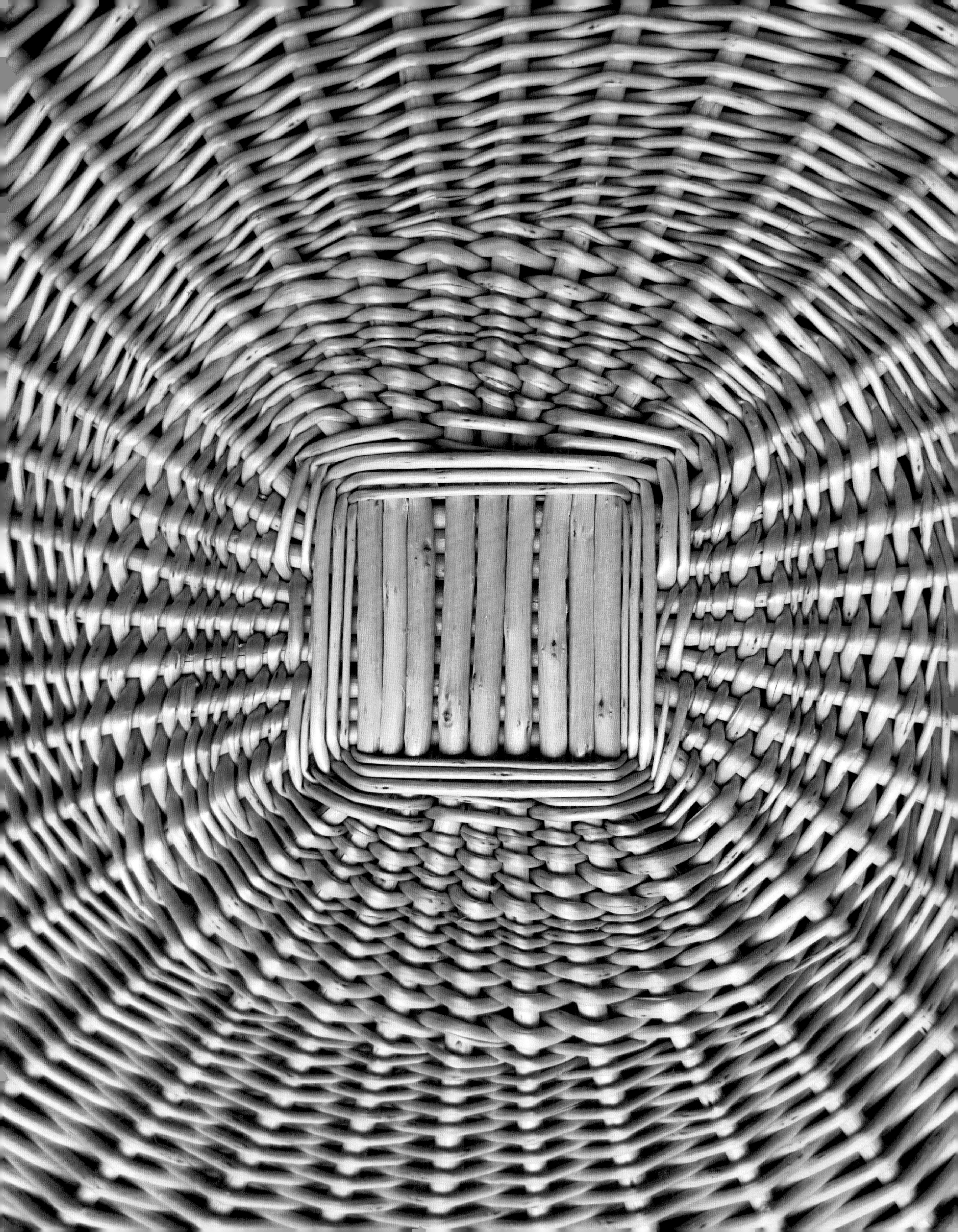

VIME STYLE

*We like rivers; for us,
they are places of escape.*

Does being born near a river shape an entire life? It would seem so, as we turn the pages of this book and are led by Benoît Rauzy, who was born a few yards from the Seine, and Anthony Watson, who grew up by the banks of the Cèze, across France to visit their homes. From Vallabrègues in Provence, whose shores are bathed by the Rhône; to Audierne Bay in Brittany, where the granite farm overlooks a coastal river; and from Paris, a stone's throw from the Seine; to the valleys of Calvados, where the lake at their Normandy house empties into the Orne River.

Rivers also play an important role in the history of Atelier Vime; they are vital for growing osier willow and provide the perfect environment for it to survive and flourish, in a world where water is an increasingly scarce resource.

Although the beauty of the natural world suffuses these places, it is not the only thing that Atelier Vime's houses have in common. They are all imbued with history, with a collector's spirit, brimming with memories and yet anchored in the present day, unlike the period rooms found in museums. Dedicated aesthetes, Anthony Watson and Benoît Rauzy see French classicism as part of a modern, living culture, whether it is the work of eighteenth-century cabinetmakers or renowned twentieth-century designers and decorators.

The two founders of Atelier Vime are knowledgeable collectors with a passion for objects and artifacts, from the most popular to the most sophisticated. The interiors that they compose adhere to their own rules. Their approach is half-instinctive, half-intellectual, drawing them "in a certain direction, through the power of placing objects side by side, over time"—an approach that inevitably finds coherence through a dialogue with the place itself. "It is clear that places have a certain spirit. We respect the genius loci. It is all a question of proportions, of high ceilings, of the realities of the space and light. Besides that, it is more out of personal curiosity that we have taken a particular interest in marbled ceramics and *indienne* fabrics in Provence; Odetta faience and Ar Seiz Breur cabinetmakers in Brittany; and, in Paris, painters and interior decorators from the interwar period, many of whom were from Central Europe and lived romantic and, sadly, tragic lives."

What defines the Vime style is the pair's ability to draw inspiration from the local artistic and decorative traditions of these places, to forge a unique identity for each of their homes in the four corners of France. These avid collectors often move paintings and other treasures from one house to another in order to complete a decor. Driven by an insatiable curiosity, they take an active interest in the chemical composition of a traditional paint, the geological specificity of a region, the quality of a fabric, or a local agricultural practice, which they combine with their impressive eye and vast knowledge of art and design history. With assured taste, they place an École d'Alger painting from the 1920s alongside a piece of rope furniture designed by Audoux-Minnet in the 1950s, or combine an eighteenth-century Aubusson tapestry with a collection of popular earthenware.

The result is clear to see in the pages of this book. These residences are replete with life and inspiration, from the smallest detail on a stair rail to the harmonious feel of an entire room. In Vallabrègues, Audierne Bay, Paris, and Normandy, the two men have created their own universe, borrowing from history, from their environment, and from the spirit of the times. In these homes, imperfections and the traces left by the passage of time play their part in enhancing the elegance of the renovations. They reflect their owners' wild dream of connecting past, present, and future, without striking a single false note.

Finding the right color with color swatches from restoration expert Élise Orrier, a specialist in natural paints and painted decorative work.

IN PROVENCE

The main road that leads to Vallabrègues is still called the "track," since it was only paved fairly recently, around twenty years ago. When they traveled along this road for the first time, Anthony Watson and Benoît Rauzy felt like they were entering a different world and another era. They still get the same feeling, even after almost twenty years. Orchards flank the river, their boughs adorned with blossom or laden with fruit, depending on the season, and cloaked in mist; horses, sheep, and cows graze in the pastures, giving the village a bucolic air, both changeable and nurturing. It is the perfect place for anyone with dreams of leading a self-sufficient life, nestled in a meander of the Rhône.

The Grand Carriero, now Rue Nationale, passes through the village from north to south. At the heart of the village stands the Hôtel Drujon, with its triple-fronted cut-stone facade framed by pilasters. The venerable old building was not looking its best when the founders of Atelier Vime purchased it. Pigeons had pecked holes in its walls, and the garden was littered with abandoned objects. Inside, the floors had been elevated to prevent flooding, and a number of doors and windows had been walled up.

Despite the gloom, the house revealed a mix of walls painted with casein, floor tiles, and imitation marble. "We liked it as it was, loaded with history and bathed in light," recalls Benoît Rauzy. "It is a beautiful building—lovely and unassuming—built by people who had good taste." The house had not been renovated for generations. Everything was worn, crooked, and had been repainted and patched up a thousand times. But the orientation, the proportions, the materials, and the spaces all held promise.

On the ground floor, the winter living room looks out onto the lane, while the summer living room—ideal for afternoon naps in the hot season—and the kitchen face onto the courtyard. In the center of the house, a large staircase with a half landing, still adorned with the traditional wrought-iron railing that is typical of Provence, leads to the bedrooms on the second floor, and continues up to the attics and, at the very top, the old dovecote.

In every room, Benoît Rauzy and Anthony Watson have preserved a trace of the past, sometimes rewriting it with the help of heritage restoration expert Élise Orrier, who oversaw the restoration of the patina on the walls and repainted the imitation marble on the doorframes and staircase. "We wanted to respect this history, to allow it to show through everywhere."

Every space features rattan and wicker furniture and accessories from their collection, which sit harmoniously alongside pieces left behind by the former owners (a demijohn, a wicker beehive, a few baskets). Next to the large, hundred-year-old acacia that shades the courtyard on sunny days, the owners have planted trees of many species, including a magnificent silk tree. In summer, they set up large tables in the shade and entertain friends by the stone basin.

Atelier Vime has gradually expanded to encompass parts of the original property that had been sold off over the years. In the early days, it was just a few privileged clients who were invited to the main house; then, after the purchase of the building on the banks of the Rhône, which had previously housed the workshops and was entirely renovated by the couple, they opened "Maison Vime" to the general public. A third annex, in the former stables, which they recently bought, will soon be home to an extension of their boutique. Today, the Hôtel Drujon has been restored to its original form, and its buildings and courtyards create a link between village life and the stunning views of the countryside and riverbanks.

A street in Vallabrègues decorated with baskets for the annual basketry festival.

THE COURTYARD AT MAISON VIME

The old facade walls are treated with a mixture of whitewash, casein, and pigments. The ground is paved using a traditional local technique, with stones taken from the riverbed of the Rhône laid vertically, which allows rainwater to run off. The courtyard was completely repaved and is now adorned with eighteenth- and nineteenth-century Anduze earthenware pots, famed for their distinctive enamel glazing, and vintage rattan chairs. Above: The Medici vase—one of Atelier Vime's first success stories; the version shown here is made of terra-cotta using the rope method, and is the result of a close collaboration with the pottery studio Le Chêne Vert.

BENEATH THE ARCHES

The house's elliptical arches are known as "basket handles" in French. The attractive blue-tinged whitewash also serves to deter insects and once protected the craftspeople who worked in the courtyard. This shade of blue is called "Guimet," after the chemist Jean-Baptiste Guimet, who invented it in 1828. Facing page: The metal garden furniture in front of the arches dates from the nineteenth century and the 1940s. Above: The space against the far wall is used for repotting plants in spring. It boasts Italian tiles and an eighteenth-century marble-top table.

THE ENTRANCE HALL

The entrance hall and the foot of the stairs set the tone: the wall shows the many-layered history of this centuries-old house. Above, left: Bundles of osier willow, waiting to be soaked and woven, stand beside an eighteenth-century marble column. Above, right: A nineteenth-century cape (from Michel Sanchez's collection) hangs above a pair of riding boots. Facing page: The lower portion of the staircase wall has been subtly restored by Élise Orrier. Hanging above the half landing is an eighteenth-century Portuguese painting.

THE SUMMER LIVING ROOM

This space was used as a dining room in the eighteenth century, then as a classroom from 1850 to 1878. Today, it is a wonderfully cool living room—perfect for entertaining friends. Facing page: The carved fountain in the corner of the room testifies to the high standing of the residence; a precursor of running water, it allowed people to drink water drawn from the outside well on the other side of the wall. Underneath the ocher-colored wash, a simple trompe-l'oeil effect, typical of eighteenth-century Provence, can be glimpsed. Above: A Provençal chemise from Fragonard and a straw hat from Jacquemus are placed on a straw-seat chair from Maison Lacroix in Vallabrègues, accompanied by sandals by Éric Bergère, a bouquet by Marie Varenne, and a collage by Mike Sajnoski.

Above: Different eras are superposed, with embroidered drapes from the late seventeenth century, a Louis XV canework chair, and an antique Braquenié fabric. Facing page: A rope lamp by Atelier Vime stands on an Atelier Martine table. An early eighteenth-century Aubusson tapestry hangs on the wall above a daybed from the French Consulate period, with pillows featuring eighteenth-century Aubusson needlepoint.

Germaine Richier

THE WINTER LIVING ROOM

Facing page: Playing with perspective between the entrance hall and the living room, which is located on the street side. An imitation marble embellishment by the restoration expert Élise Orrier frames the door; in the background, an eighteenth-century English painting of Lord Cavendish hangs above a sideboard from the same period, on which are placed nineteenth-century ewers from Çanakkale, in Turkey.
Above: A view of the living room, with the Aramis ceiling light by Atelier Vime, a sofa by Jules Leleu, cushions by Drusus Tabor, a rug by Paule Leleu, and, seen from the back, an armchair by Ico Parisi. On the right are two rope armchairs designed by Audoux-Minnet; in the background, a lamp by Max Ingrand stands on an eighteenth-century Spanish desk.

Facing page: In the living room, above the mantel, is a painting from 1926 by Henri Chevalier, who belonged to the École d'Alger (a movement that Benoît Rauzy is especially fond of), alongside a candle in a small terra-cotta Medici vase by Atelier Vime and wall lamps from the 1940s. Above, left: A detail of a sideboard by Audoux-Minnet with a raffia embellishment, and Atelier Vime's Edith lamp. Above, right: A Florence Knoll sideboard stands beneath a group of paintings from the 1920s and 1930s by Charles Dufresne, Gerd Arntz, Mathieu Rosianu, and Ernest Engel-Pak, one of the first abstract painters.

THE KITCHEN

This room is the heart of the home, where everyone gathers for meals, but also to chat, read, work, draw, and, of course, cook. The kitchen has retained its character thanks to the original flagstone floor, which was discovered underneath tons of rubble. Facing page: Atelier Vime's Gabriel lampshade hangs from the ceiling. Above: Benoît Rauzy and Anthony Watson have assembled a collection of tablecloths and place mats that reflects their passion for table settings and entertaining; the Eye place mats and Medici vase complement plates by Gavin Houghton, and antique glasses and water whistles.

Faience collection

Driven by their own tastes as much as by their family heritage, Anthony Watson and Benoît Rauzy collect faience—tin-glazed earthenware—especially pieces from Moustiers. Below, left: An eighteenth-century fluted plate. Below, right: A Moustiers plate. Facing page: An eighteenth-century Louis XV dresser, displaying faience from the same period.

THE STAIRCASE

Facing page: The staircase leading up to the third floor from the second-floor landing, with its original blue walls, well-trodden steps, and wrought-iron railing. The staircases in many local houses, from the most humble to the most sophisticated, are adorned with these scrolled railings. On the half landing, Benoît Rauzy and Anthony Watson have placed a pair of tall wooden corner cupboards dating to the period when the house was built. The row of five windows, situated 25 feet (8 meters) above the ground, bathe the staircase in light. Above: The second-floor landing serves several bedrooms; here, those on the west side lead to the large balcony.

THE BLUE BEDROOM

This bedroom is the largest room in the house. On the wall it shares with the bathroom are displayed works of embroidery (the one on the bottom left, from the Galerie Bernard Durand in L'Isle-sur-la-Sorgue, depicts a basket-maker), a drawing of a bullfight by Jean Cocteau, and a nude by André Derain. The Medici vase on the chest of drawers has been painted green—the result of a collaboration with Farrow & Ball. The tomette tiled floor is original. The basket that can be glimpsed in the bathroom was found in the house's old workshops.

Facing page: The canopy bed features a Braquenié fabric and a quilted eighteenth-century cover from Michel Sanchez's collection. Above: The ceiling beams have retained their original gray color. On the mantel, a portrait by Charles Kvapil is placed alongside a drawing by Wayne Pate, and a seventeenth-century Persian vase stands proudly on the pedestal table. The fireplace hearth is decorated with a collection of basketwork from Atelier Vime's archives. An eighteenth-century child's chair and a lyre-back armchair by Martin Julien complete the room's decor.

ANTIQUE TEXTILES

Whether antique, vintage, reedited, or contemporary, made locally or brought back from trips abroad, fabrics have pride of place in Atelier Vime's homes. Facing page: In front of the fireplace, a late seventeenth-century Imberline fabric, and to the right, an eighteenth-century embroidered fabric from Turkey. Above, left: The Braquenié fabric on the canopy bed. Above, right: A wall hanging depicting the family tree of a Provençal family.

Color palettes

Benoît Rauzy and Anthony Watson decided to keep most of the original colors on the walls, sometimes restoring them with the help of Élise Orrier. She applied a patina created using traditional local pigments, especially blue—this color was used outdoors to keep mosquitoes at bay, while indoors its purpose was purely decorative.

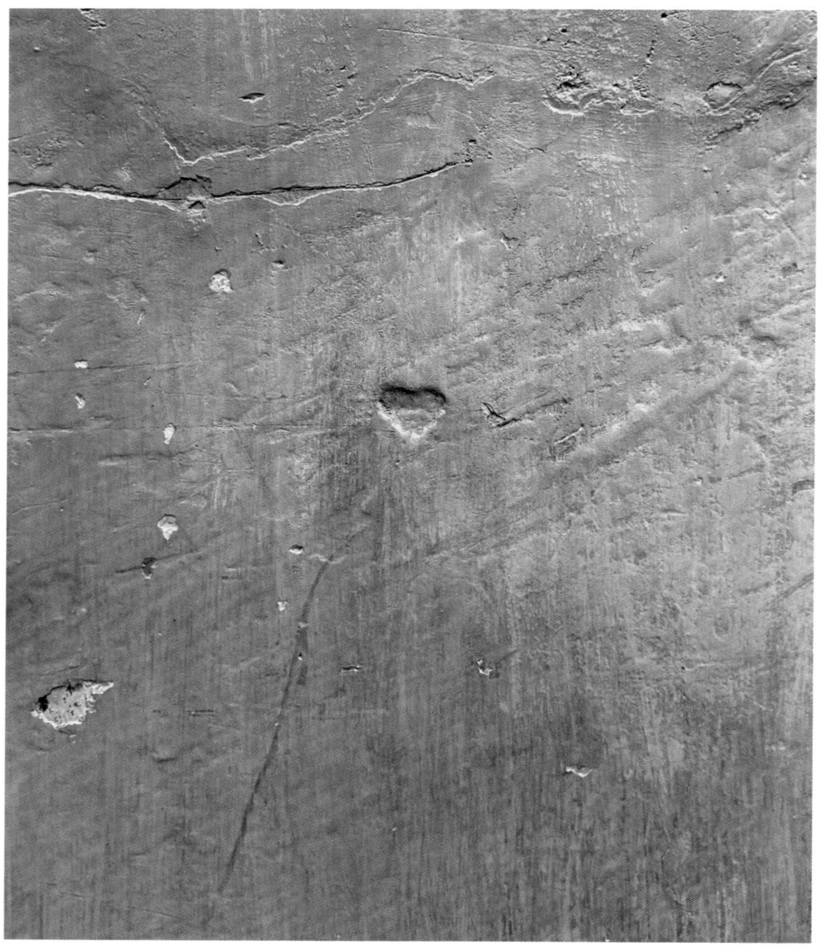

THE GUEST BEDROOM

In this bedroom, the ceilings have been left almost untouched, while the walls have been repainted in the original colors. The eighteenth- and nineteenth-century quilted covers are taken from various collections, and, on the floor, a Persian rug with a boteh pattern dates from 1830. Above: An Audoux-Minnet lamp and a Louis XV chaise longue.

This house reveals manifold perspectives, such as these two interconnecting bedrooms on the west side. Anthony Watson and Benoît Rauzy reopened some of the doorways that had been walled up in order to restore the original layout; the framing is accentuated by painted eighteenth-century decorations placed above the doors. Braquenié drapes shield the rooms from the strong southern sun. Above: A large Medici vase holding a floral display by Marie Varenne adds a touch of color to the space. Facing page: A Louis XV chaise longue has been reupholstered in a fabric dyed using a traditional French technique known as *chiné à la branche*, sourced from Jérôme Prévost, an antique fabric specialist based in Tarascon. In front of the fireplace stands an eighteenth-century earthenware stove.

THE LANDING

Remaining faithful to the spirit of the eighteenth century, Benoît Rauzy and Anthony Watson have decorated the landing as if it were a room in its own right. Here, a framed detail from a piece of antique wallpaper is displayed on a Louis XV table.

THE BATHROOM

Facing page: A cozy corner in which to relax, the bathroom is decorated with Braquenié fabric on the far wall. It features a nineteenth-century bathtub in copper—a material that conserves the heat of the water—above which hangs an eighteenth-century portrait of a woman. Above: A rattan mirror from the 1960s.

Ewer collection

Çanakkale ewers were made in the eponymous city in Turkey, to export raki to Provence, particularly to the towns of Beaucaire and Avignon. Locals called them "demoiselles d'Avignon." Facing page: Çanakkale ewers stand on a Louis XV console table alongside a nineteenth-century Turkish vase in which Benoît Rauzy has placed a bouquet of wildflowers gathered from around the house. This is a passion he indulges at each of their properties, skillfully composing colorful flower arrangements to decorate various rooms.

AT THE HEART OF MAISON VIME

In this bedroom, the original blue color of the walls has been preserved. Above, left: The chairs are by Les Artisans de Marolles, Jean Royère, and Mathieu Matégot. Above, right: The room features a canopy bed by Atelier Vime, with antique linen sheets, as well as an eighteenth-century Provençal armchair and drapes by Colefax & Fowler. Facing page: A Medici vase and vase sconce, and a Beaucaire table (all by Atelier Vime) complement a Louis XV armchair. Over the door hang eighteenth-century plates from Marseille. The drapes were designed by Pierre Frey and the fabric on the ceiling is by Brigitte Singh.

THE ATTIC BEDROOMS

Under the roof, bathed in light, the old attics overlook the Rhône and, beyond the river, the Abbey of Saint Roman, a cave monastery. The original floor tiles have been preserved. Facing page: A canopy bed by Atelier Vime features a block-print fabric by Brigitte Singh and a quilted cover from the reign of Louis Philippe. The bed perfectly complements the 1945 painting of a nude by Margaret Cossaceanu; on the floor stand Italian stools from the 1940s. Above: Two single beds made of rattan, from the 1960s, are placed beneath a papier-mâché bull's head by Claude Samson, an artist who moved to Vallabrègues in the 1960s.

One of the bedrooms affords a panoramic view of the terrace and garden, beautifully framed by drapes in a Braquenié fabric.

Hidden traces

Below, left and facing page: Details of some of the house's original painted decoration. Naive paintings of imitation marble—a typical effect used in Provence during the eighteenth century—sometimes covered the walls of entire rooms; these were discovered beneath paint dating from the nineteenth century. Below, right: Pieces of graffiti, scattered throughout a number of rooms, have been preserved as testaments to the history of the residence. A notable example was in the former dovecote, where the date of every important event in the life of the family was recorded. The text reads, "Marius Boyer père [father], Aramis Boyer, Ollivier Boyer, l'an de la paix [the year of peace] 1918."

THE STUDIO

The former attic, which held the house's archives when the property was purchased, has been turned into the design studio—a workshop under the roof. Today, antique pieces sit harmoniously alongside Atelier Vime's creations. The organized chaos recounts the history of wickerwork and reveals how Benoît Rauzy and Anthony Watson have succeeded in breathing new life into it. Although they create their own new designs, they also draw inspiration from traditional weaving techniques.

PAGES 96 AND 97:
The Giens Peninsula, in Provence.
The Pointe du Millier, in Brittany.

IN BRITTANY

Atelier Vime was born at the heart of the Rhône delta, but it is in Audierne Bay, just before the promontory of the Pointe du Raz, that Anthony Watson and Benoît Rauzy decided to plant their own crop of osier willow, writing a new chapter in the company's story.

This former farm was purchased by Benoît Rauzy's parents as a vacation home in the early 1960s, before city-dwellers began to flock to the region. It is in a quiet backwater of Brittany, a wild place where vacationers still don't venture, despite the beauty of the coast: with its clear waters, sandy beaches, and coves interspersed with granite cliffs topped by colorful moors, it forms a magnificent, deserted landscape.

Driven by a passion for art and the environment, Benoît Rauzy and Anthony Watson have insisted that Atelier Vime's designs be made using osier willow that has not been treated with chemicals. And the best way to ensure the feasibility of this demand was to try it themselves, which is how they came to revive an ancient local tradition, with the help of Gaël Davoli, a landscape gardener who lives in the area. Thus, the osier willow plantation in Finistère was born. Osier willow had previously been cultivated across large parts of this region, where farmers spent the long winters weaving baskets for gathering the harvests, as well as traps for fishermen in the nearby ports of Le Guilvinec and Douarnenez. This kind of basketwork, which uses a curved frame for weaving, is unique to Brittany; it is a distinct piece of intangible cultural heritage within Europe that, unfortunately, no longer forms part of a basket-maker's standard training in France.

Today, it is here, in this former day laborer's house—a small seventeenth-century building where the workers used to live, across from the farmhouse—that the osier willow is left to dry. The harvest is then brought into the former barn, a workshop that is attached to the house, where the branches are sorted and prepared for weaving.

Inside the old farmhouse, Anthony Watson and Benoît Rauzy have drawn on their unrivaled talent for combining different styles and eras, while respecting the genius loci: the sofa in the summer living room was designed by Benoît's father, a dentist by profession, and the staircase and door frames are decorated with the same paint that was used for fishing boats, which have long since been supplanted by pleasure boats in Audierne's harbor. Much of the furniture is from the Ar Seiz Breur movement, an avant-garde collective that was active in Brittany in the 1920s and 1930s. Its style is echoed in the modern ceramics by Odetta, named after the Odet River, which flows through Quimper. Works by Breton painters such as Henri Rivière, Max Jacob, and Louis Marie Désiré Lucas are placed alongside those by artists who passed through at one time or another: Nina Nidermiller and her teacher André Lhote, the Provençal artists Albert Gleizes and Paule Fournel, Micheline Catty, and Wayne Pate. Postwar modernist pieces, such as a large rug by André Arbus and armchairs by Audoux-Minnet, complete the decor in this house that is strewn with piles of books and creations by Atelier Vime.

The consciously eclectic feel by no means distorts the buildings' agricultural origins, or the bohemian spirit that Benoît Rauzy's parents brought to them. The farmhouse, which has retained the air of a family home, has become a laboratory for osier willow and its many varieties. Yet it remains a place full of life, where successive generations come to preserve their predecessors' commitment to art and nature.

A view of Rue Chère in the village of Pont-Croix.

THE WALLED GARDEN

The old stable forms one of the walls around the farmyard, which extends toward the former day laborer's house and other agricultural buildings. It was part of the original farm, before the house was rebuilt in the nineteenth century, as can be seen from its traditional curved lintel, carved into the granite (facing page). Above: This former outhouse has been transformed into a walled vegetable garden with a seating area sheltered from the wind; it features a rattan bench from 1960, covered with an Uzbek *suzani* textile that Benoît Rauzy brought back from a trip abroad. Atelier Vime planters sit alongside two large metal pots planted with olive trees, designed by Hervé Baume.

THE BARN AND FIELDS

A holistic approach has been adopted for the garden, which is considered in its entirety.
Above: Anthony Watson and Gaël Davoli, a local landscape gardener, harvest lavender plants that play a key role in pollination and serve to deter aphids. Facing page: The hydrangeas, which were planted here in the 1960s, bloom alongside hibiscus, creating a rural idyll.

PAGES 104–105:
A view of the north facade. Closed off on their west side to protect them from strong winds, houses in Brittany traditionally have very small windows on their north facade. Here, the windows were created in the 1960s, using traditional materials.

THE SUMMER GARDEN

Tables are set up in various parts of the garden, depending on the time of day and the light.
Facing page: Garden chairs by Mathieu Matégot—the iconic postwar designer of metal furniture—are placed in the osier willow field in the glow of the setting sun, ready for a bucolic aperitif; the wicker and leather tray on the table was designed by Atelier Vime for Diptyque.

THE KITCHEN

Above: Displayed on the wall is a rare collection of painted plates from 1922–1923 by Suzanne and René-Yves Creston, members of the avant-garde Ar Seiz Breur movement, which combined art deco motifs with a Breton aesthetic. This ensemble, hanging above a backsplash of antique Italian tiles, was created thanks to the collaboration of Tangui Le Lonquer. Facing page: Atelier Vime's signature blend of styles can be seen here, with a 1930s rattan chair, an Atelier Vime ceiling light, and a ceramic compote dish by Paul Yvain, a Breton ceramist from the 1950s.

THE DINING ROOM

The dining room's focal point is a seventeenth-century Louis XIII table, which stands on a Codimat rug made from woven natural fibers. Facing page: In the background, on the Florence Knoll sideboard, Atelier Vime's LP2 lamp, a drawing by Léopold Survage on the right, and Breton ceramics by Odetta form part of Anthony Watson and Benoît Rauzy's personal collection. Above: A Raku bowl and a family teapot rub shoulders with a 1960s Audoux-Minnet rattan chair upholstered in a fabric designed by Élise Djo-Bourgeois for Pierre Frey and custom dyed by Atelier Vime.

THE FORMER STABLES

Different motifs are combined in this room, with a tapestry by François Planeix—a weaver from Uzel in the Côtes d'Armor département, and a member of the Ar Seiz Breur movement from 1937—paired with a Codimat rug made of woven fibers. Two sofas by Yves Halard make this an inviting space to sit and talk or to read; on the wall hangs a 1930s painting by Mathieu Rosianu.

Tiny basket collection

Anthony Watson and Benoît Rauzy collect tiny baskets from all over France. These traditional pieces were made by apprentices training for their exams, as an exercise to test their basketry skills. Displayed on a Verdure Aubusson tapestry from the eighteenth century (below) or gathered together in a seventeenth-century buffet along with rustic eighteenth-century plates (facing page), they all have a particular use. They were found by the couple, or were given to them by friends.

THE LIVING ROOM

In the past, small benches provided seating inside the huge granite hearth with its wooden lintel. Anthony Watson and Benoît Rauzy wanted to preserve the rustic feel and the simplicity of the house. A brightly colored rug by André Arbus and a velvet sofa designed by Benoît Rauzy's father bring a touch of warmth to the room. A Louis Sognot easy chair sits on the left, and in the foreground are two Audoux-Minnet armchairs. The wicker pelmets are by Atelier Vime and the drapes were sewn from old sheets.

SAVINA TAKES PRIDE OF PLACE

Facing page: The solid oak armchair was designed in 1947 by Joseph Savina, a cabinetmaker from Tréguier. In 1930, he met Le Corbusier, who would have a profound influence on his work, and he went on to collaborate with the architect on a series of wooden sculptures. The mahogany table was created between 1935 and 1945 by Jorj Rual, a cabinetmaker from Rennes who was also a member of the Ar Seiz Breur movement. A piece of forged iron traditionally used as currency in Cameroon and an LP lamp are placed on the table. Above: The small hallway provides direct access to the north-facing garden.

THE BATHROOM

In the bathroom, the sink and faucets are from the art deco period and the sconce is by Atelier Vime. The mosaic on the floor is inspired by the work of Isidore Odorico, a mosaic artist from Rennes. Facing page: The bathroom is furnished in wicker, with a Paquebot rattan armchair by Atelier Vime; the block-printed drapes are by Drusus Tabor.

UPSTAIRS

Facing page: In the bedroom, on the original elmwood floor, a bookcase made from planks of wood and bricks forms the backdrop for an Empire armchair draped with an Uzbek *suzani* fabric. Above: The tiny central bedroom is laid out like a ship's cabin, with a scalloped pelmet and a bedspread made from a Provençal skirt sourced from Alain Le Berre. A stool by Germaine Darbois-Gaudin, designed in 1949 for the ocean liner *Île-de-France*, has been converted into a bedside table.

FAMILY MEMENTOS

Above: A portrait of Ossip Zadkine and an ink drawing of a Harlequin by Jean Boulet. Facing page: A nineteenth-century kilim rug, a chair by Jean Lachaud, and a farm table used as a desk. A Breton basket has been turned into a wastepaper basket. The pelmet is by Atelier Vime and on the bookshelves in the background is a watercolor by Nikolai Dronnikov. The shelves are overflowing with books accumulated over the years.

CENTURIES OF DECORATIVE ART

In front of the hearth stands an antique stove in faience, with, on the left, a 1960s floor lamp by an unknown designer and, on the right, a Directoire-era bench. In the foreground, an Uzbek *suzani* fabric can be glimpsed on the bed.

PAGES 128–129:

IN THE ATTIC

Tucked away at the top of the house, away from the hustle and bustle, the summer bedroom looks like a stage set. It has a canopy bed that is perfect for napping, covered with antique fabrics—hemp sheets and an eighteenth-century Aubusson tapestry—and surrounded by hundreds of books. In the background stands an eighteenth-century Malouine wardrobe (from Saint-Malo). In the foreground, an Audoux-Minnet lamp with a lampshade by Décors Barbares sits on a small Indo-Portuguese table from Gujarat, with a bouquet of hydrangeas from the garden placed on the floor.

THE OUTBUILDING

Dating from the seventeenth century, the small outbuilding is the oldest construction on the farm. It has been left untouched, including its rammed earth floor. Osier wil.ow is placed here to dry, beneath the swallows' nests. Above: A raw wicker beehive created with Gaël Davoli.

THE OSIER WILLOW FIELD

The field is mainly planted with petite grisette (*Salix triandra*), also known as almond-leaved willow—a variety that is well suited to making small objects. The apple orchard is a traditional feature in Breton gardens, and the fruit trees are regularly replaced.

PAGES 134–135:
The sound, which lies just below the farm, meanders for a few miles before rejoining the coast. It swells and empties with the tides. Reminiscent of a childhood den, a rustic pergola is set up alongside a dinner table, in the light of the setting sun on a summer's evening.

IN PARIS

In the early 1950s—1953 to be exact—Benoît Rauzy's father moved into an apartment on Rue des Saints-Pères. This street links Saint-Germain-des-Prés—the intellectual, student, and party district, full of jazz clubs, cafés, and galleries—to Faubourg Saint-Germain (the area around the Basilica of Saint Clotilde), the last bastion of the aristocracy, where a certain Proustian spirit still lingers in the air. While the nearby stores were mainly occupied by antique dealers, there were still a few workshops tucked away in the courtyards. People lived in Saint-Germain-des-Prés, not for the luxury, but for the culture.

The apartment on Rue des Saints-Pères was full of books and paintings, some left behind by artist friends who had stayed there for a few months in the servants' quarters on the seventh floor. Benoît Rauzy's walk to school was a rite of passage in itself. The first gallerists that he encountered as a child were, among others, the voluptuous and vivacious Dina Vierny—a former model for Matisse and Maillol—whose gravelly voice could be heard belting out songs from Kolyma; Madeleine Castaing, a renowned interior designer also known as the "woman with the elastic" (a reference to the elastic strap tucked under her chin that simultaneously kept her wig in place and restored her face to the taut, perfectly oval shape of her youth); and Gilles Bernard at the Galerie Proscenium, a small but extraordinary place that exhibited works by Christian Bérard, Erté (Romain de Tirtoff), Tom Keogh, and others long before the market showed any interest in these artists.

The apartment in which Anthony Watson and Benoît Rauzy live today still retains this ambiance. As you walk from room to room, it feels as if you are turning the pages of a book: your gaze alights first on the parquet floors and period floor tiles, then on a painting by Anton Räderscheidt, a German artist who was a member of the New Objectivity movement. In this vast duplex apartment on the top floors of an early eighteenth-century building, a collection of old books is at home beside drawings by Pablo Picasso and Eugène Boudin, as well as a display of marbled ceramic plates from Apt.

"And while their home occasionally serves as their Paris showroom, meaning that Rauzy and Watson regularly swap out new designs and discoveries, the place still evokes a bygone city," Laura May Todd wrote in a *New York Times* article published on November 30, 2022. Because, although the area has clearly changed a lot since the 1950s and the subsequent era when Benoît Rauzy was a student at Sciences Po, just a few streets away, the spirit of those times can still be felt in this apartment. Just like their homes in Provence, Brittany, and Normandy, it is imbued with a touch of magic.

The eighteenth-century stairwell leading up to the apartment has retained its original floor tiles; it showcases a Medici vase and pedestal—Atelier Vime's signature design.

THE LIVING ROOM

At the end of a long row of adjoining rooms, the living room is bathed in light. Anthony Watson and Benoît Rauzy place their current favorite pieces of furniture here for a while before they put them up for sale, creating ephemeral, discerning decors. Here, an easy chair and matching daybed attributed to Louis Sognot and a stool by André Sornay, upholstered in a Fortuny fabric, are arranged around a table designed by Jacques Adnet and made by metalworker Gilbert Poillerat. On the floor is a Codimat rug, and in the background an antique scrolled guardrail serves as a decorative object. A painting of a café terrace in summertime by Anton Räderscheidt and two heads in terra-cotta and plaster by the Catalan artist Josep Clara provide the finishing touches.

UNEXPECTED ENCOUNTERS

In the living room, a chest from the Haute Époque (a term that refers to pieces from the Middle Ages, Renaissance, and early Baroque period) is illuminated by an Atelier Vime rope lamp. On the left, a daybed by Louis Sognot stands on the original chevron parquet floor, and, on the right, a Louis XV armchair can be seen. This room epitomizes the pair's talent for combining different styles and eras.

SUISSE ROMANE
TOURAINE ROMANE
POITOU ROMAN
AUVERGNE ROMANE
L'ART CISTERCIEN
ROUSSILLON ROMAN
CATALOGNE ROMANE
CATALOGNE ROMANE
DE GRECO À PICASSO
POUSSIN
REMBRANDT

Painting, drawing, and sculpture collection

Benoît Rauzy has a passion for art and collects paintings and drawings from the 1910s to the 1930s. His finds can be seen in various arrangements throughout the apartment. Below, left: A work by Wayne Pate is displayed alongside drawings by Jean Cocteau, Pablo Picasso, and Léopold Survage. Below, right: A costume design by Pavel Tchelitchev for Jean Giraudoux's *Ondine*. Facing page: A sketch of a woman in a leotard by Charles Despiau is placed on the floor beside a rattan table with a bust by Margaret Cossaceanu, a Romanian sculptor who trained under Antoine Bourdelle.

THE SPIRIT OF VIME

Above: In an ode to simplicity, a bird sculpture by brothers Jean and Joël Martel and a rope lamp by Atelier Vime are showcased on a seventeenth-century table. The table is framed by two brutalist chairs and an ink portrait by Ossip Zadkine. Facing page: Astute color choices reflect the eclectic mix of eras: beige and brown in the round rug by Paule Leleu and the woven rope sofa designed by Giuseppe Pagano, or the mahogany chair by Djo Bourgeois that complements the red on the walls of the study in the background. In the study, a Tit Mellil chair by Mathieu Matégot, designed in 1955 for Casablanca Airport, provides a counterpoint to the formalism of a rustic desk from the Louis XVI era.

PAGES 146–147:

THE STUDY

Bookshelves were built into the alcoves formed by the old chimney flues that passed through the study's walls. Here, again, is another eclectic mix of genres with a Louis XVI desk, a chair by Charlotte Perriand, a Kadjar lamp, and, placed on the stool, a photograph by Jacques Léonard, from the Anne Clergue Galerie.

Rodtchenko
ENSOR
SCHIELE
PRADO
BOTTICELLI
FABERGÉ
PARIS
MOSCOU

Book collection

Each of their houses demonstrates the same taste for combining pieces from different eras, as well as a love of books—antiquarian books, literature, fine art books—like a common thread running through their homes. Below: Among the numerous copies sits a photo of Anthony Watson and Alma, their Podenco Andaluz warren hound, by Philippe Sardin. Facing page: Beneath a drawing by Édouard Manet, a small desk by Jean Caumont holds books from Juliette Gréco's library.

THE DINING ROOM

Above: The space leading to the dining room is decorated with both antique and contemporary artworks, with a mural by Wayne Pate behind a Medici vase and pedestal. Facing page: The dining room blends the classicism of a marquetry chest of drawers and furniture by Eero Saarinen with two caricatures from the 1940s and a black hemp rug by Codimat.

THE WICKER ANTEROOM

Providing an interlude of sorts, this small room features a wall covered in wicker panels by Atelier Vime and marbled ceramic plates from Uzès. It takes on different looks and purposes, depending on the moment or the occasion. Here, it forms the anteroom to the dining room, and also serves as a cosy TV lounge. The Beaucaire stools have been upholstered in a Décors Barbares fabric. Above, left: A detail of the wicker panels and Edith lamp by Atelier Vime. Above, right: Atelier Vime's LP lamp.

Marbled ceramic collection

Anthony Watson, whose mother is from Provence, has always known his family to collect ceramics, especially marbled pottery—a passion that he has also inherited. They may look identical from a distance, but in reality each piece is unique. He is particularly fond of nineteenth-century items made by Maison Pichon in Uzès. Facing page: A fabric by Décors Barbares provides the perfect backdrop for pieces from the collection.

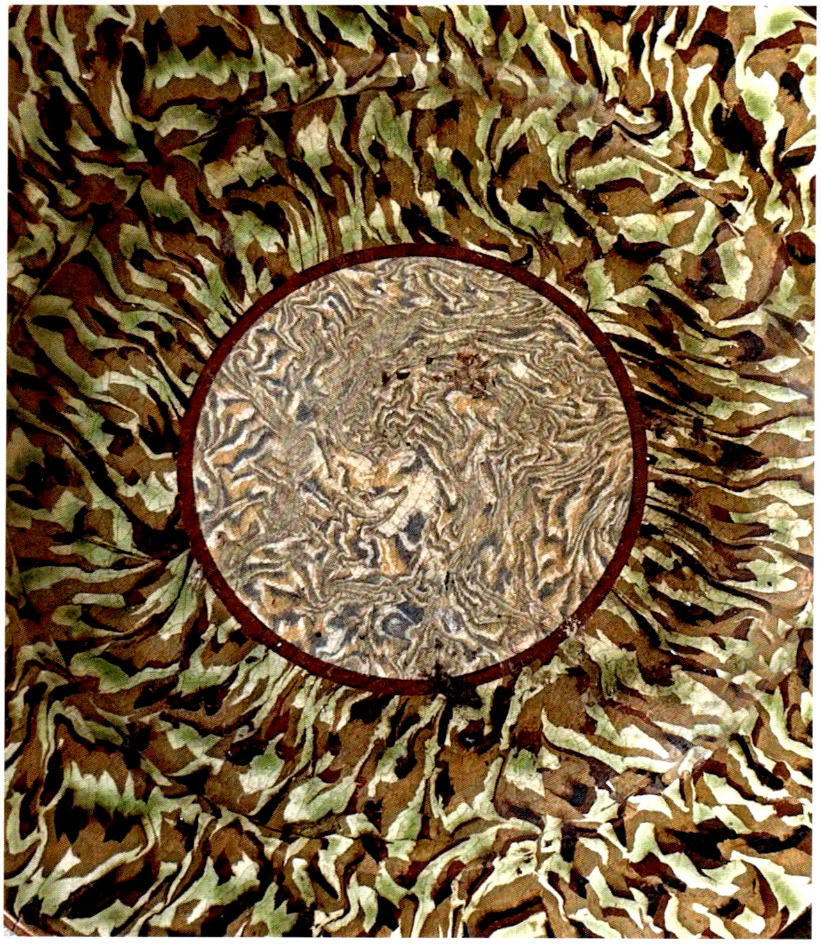

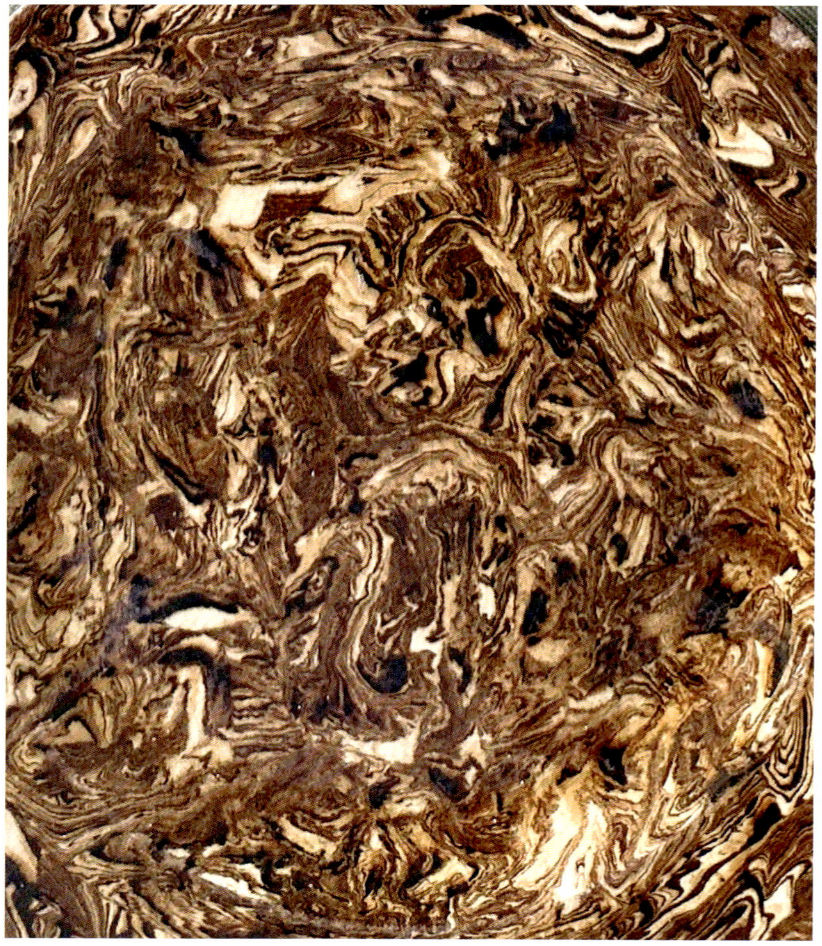

THE KITCHEN

Benoît Rauzy and Anthony Watson have gone for a total green look in the kitchen, with paint by Farrow & Ball, a carpet by Codimat, and a glass lamp by Audoux-Minnet, infusing the room with an air that is at once English and Provençal. The small square table is also by Audoux-Minnet. Created for the tennis club in Villefranche-sur-Mer, the chair is by Harry Bertoïa, and the backsplash is a design by Andrée Putman for Bisazza. The sconce, in the shape of a banana leaf, is an Atelier Vime creation.

RHEIN UND MAAS
LES REALISMES

THE ATTIC BEDROOMS

The open spaces and original features of the servants' rooms have been preserved in the attic bedrooms, where artist friends often stayed. Facing page: A large rattan easy chair by Louis Sognot and a tree stump (probably left over from the construction of the building's structural framework) used as a coffee table and holding an Odetta vase. To the left of the doorway, a self-portrait by Pierre Bompard, who was Peintre de la Marine (official painter of the fleet), is displayed, and, on the right, a lampshade by Wayne Pate can be seen. In the background are chairs by Roger Landault. Above: In the study area, eighteenth-century armchairs stand in front of the hearth, with an Atelier Vime potholder on the mantel. Among the works on the wall are *Le Tailleur* by Max Jacob, a drawing by Natalia Goncharova, and a watercolor by Alexandre Benois.

THE BEDROOM

This bedroom on the seventh floor boasts a view over the rooftops of Paris that stretches as far as the Grand Palais and the Eiffel Tower. Above: Through the doorway, the Edith lamp by Atelier Vime can be glimpsed. Facing page: An Atelier Vime mirror hangs on the wall, and an Uzbek *suzani* fabric, which Benoît Rauzy brought back from one of his many trips, covers the bed.

PAGES 162 AND 163:
The Vime bag is showcased beside a seated nude sculpture by Charles Despiau; above them hangs an ink portrait by Ossip Zadkine. Alma, the Podenco Andaluz, poses in front of the desk.

IN NORMANDY

Perched on a hillside overlooking the valley of the Orne River, the château is built of Caen stone and is nine windows wide, framed by pilasters and crowned by a wide pediment. It boasts an English garden surrounded by meadows and forest. The young roebuck and the waterbirds that greeted Anthony Watson and Benoît Rauzy on their first visit are still here, as are the pheasants that nest in the tall grasses of the park—the true lords of the manor. A grove of lilacs, some antique rosebushes, a few rhododendrons, and a cluster of camellias are the only remnants of the former flowerbeds that provided the bucolic backdrop to an aristocratic life shaped by ancestral traditions. Nature has reclaimed the space, wild plants have grown over the vast vegetable garden, yet there remain a few traces of where paths and perspectives were once meticulously outlined: a row of poplars here, centuries-old lime trees and oaks there.

The house is typical of the summer residences known in French as "houses of the fields," where aristocratic and bourgeois families from Caen and Bayeux came to enjoy the countryside. In classic eighteenth-century style, light and air stream into the huge dual-aspect rooms, providing a haven for private and family life.

Built during Louis XV's reign in the early eighteenth century, the house had lost none of its soul, despite the ravages of time. The decorative domino paper lining a cupboard, the elegant wrought-iron banister on the central staircase, the shells that decorate the stone mantels, as well as the humble dwelling of the gardener, the estate's former bakery, all sparked the two men's imaginations, and they quickly set to work. In the midst of this unspoiled countryside, where the only people to be seen are walkers, the duo knew that Atelier Vime had found a new setting for its creations.

The renovation work got underway, following the same approach as always: getting rid of incongruous additions; restoring the original layout; preserving the patina on the walls, the weathering of the stone, and the creaking of the woodwork. For a house, these features are like the wrinkles on a face—the external expression of the memories they hold.

In the main courtyard, which had been neglected for fifteen years, the old well that provided water for a pond and the gardens was made functional once again, thanks to an expert's magic touch. The pond was cleaned up, and the area around it became a wetland rich in biodiversity. Anthony Watson and Benoît Rauzy worked with a genealogist to discover the origins of the estate and the history of how it was passed down, learning about the familial, cultural, and economic ties between the château, the land, and the surrounding region. That is how they discovered that a certain Mademoiselle Putecotte de Reneville, who owned land all the way to the coast, received an annual rent from her tenant farmers paid in butter and oysters! Successive chatelains—through noble honors, positions, and strategic marriages—were able to rise in status, while always returning to their rural Normandy setting: Jean-Charles Guillaume Le Vaillant was head page to King Louis XVI; Luc Alen, an Irish-born count and husband of Marie Charlotte de Béhague, took part in the conquest of the Indies. These men are no longer here, but they are proof of the château's link to the royal court and to major events of the time. These noble links continue today: bed sheets are still made from a kind of traditional Normandy linen known as "blue gold" that young women learn to embroider in Bayeux stitch, which—in the words of Charles Germain de Saint-Aubin, embroidery designer to King Louis XV—is like painting with a needle.

Naturally, the two collectors began hunting down and buying furniture well before they had signed the real estate contract. Siamoise, Imberline, *chiné à la branche* (a traditional French silk-dyeing technique)—the names of antique fabrics echoed off the bare walls that they were destined to adorn. Furniture and objects were temporarily placed in rooms to gain a sense of the dimensions and the play of light. Raphaelle Hanley's watercolors capture the project as a work-in-progress, as its shape starts to emerge, like a pointillist painting.

Since their acquisition, Anthony Watson and Benoît Rauzy have endeavored to breathe new life into the château by renovating the building and its surroundings, but also by drawing on its three centuries of history to write the next chapter in its story and to restore its soul.

At the foot of the hill, one of the many streams that run through the wooded Normandy countryside can be seen from the château.

PANORAMIC VIEW

The main courtyard undergoing renovations. As with all of their houses, Anthony Watson and Benoît Rauzy were not afraid to take on major restoration work in order to give the château a new lease of life.

"The most beautiful of its places for me was the hollow of a valley by the side of fresh water, in the shade of willows."

Gaston Bachelard, *Water and Dreams*

STAIRCASE AND DUAL-ASPECT VIEW

The floor of the stairwell, made of Caen stone, complements the finely worked wrought-iron banister from the Louis XV era. Facing page: The view from the front to the back of the house demonstrates the typical layout of these summer homes, which usually open onto both the main courtyard and the gardens.

ENDURING MEMORIES

Above: The domino wallpaper (decorative wood-block or hand-printed prints) that lined alcoves, cupboards, and sometimes entire rooms, has been laid bare. Facing page: One of the bedrooms overlooking the gardens, with its floor, fireplace, and trumeau above the mantel in Caen stone, is in the process of being renovated. In order for Benoît Rauzy and Anthony Watson to envisage how the space will look, a few pieces of furniture have been placed here provisionally, such as this daybed from the French Regency period draped with an eighteenth-century Siamoise fabric from Normandy. Here, as elsewhere, the couple have immersed themselves in the atmosphere of the place and combined the Vime style with furniture and fabrics from the local area.

Antique fabric collection

Pairs of shoes dating from the 1840s to 1850s were found in the attic and have been placed by Anthony Watson in fine wickerwork baskets from Atelier Vime's archives. For the founders of Atelier Vime, every new setting is a playground and a place for experimentation. Facing page: An eighteenth-century jacket embroidered with flowers.

Above: Imberline fabric from the late seventeenth century.
Facing page: Eighteenth-century Imerbline fabric dyed using the *chiré à la branche* technique.

THE DINING ROOM

To help them imagine the space, Anthony Watson and Benoît Watson asked Raphaelle Hanley to paint preparatory studies of the rooms with their intended decors. This watercolor shows the dining room, with a collection of eighteenth-century engravings by François-Nicolas Martinet, recalling the Count of Buffon's cabinet of curiosities in Montbard.

THE SMALL LIVING ROOM

This painting illustrates the couple's idea of combining an Italian sofa from the 1960s with antique pieces, beneath the exposed beams of the small living room. The eighteenth-century decorative features above the doorways come from Marshal Joseph Joffre's final residence in Louveciennes.

Thanks to Jean-Pierre, who has worked his magic, and to Vincent, who is overseeing the renovation work, the well in the courtyard has been rediscovered. It will be used to fill the pond, which had long since disappeared. On the right stands a small tower set into the surrounding stone wall—a typical feature of these kinds of eighteenth-century residences.

PAGES 182 AND 183:
A fireplace mantel bearing Benoît Rauzy's first bouquet arranged in this new house. One of the château's bedrooms, with an eighteenth-century fire screen and an Aubusson rug from the Restoration period.

FROM DESIGN TO DECOR

In 2016, Anthony Watson and Benoît Rauzy founded the Atelier Vime design studio, where all of their collections are conceived. Soon after, they were joined by their friend Raphaelle Hanley, who had many years' experience as an artistic director designing leather goods for luxury brands, both in France and internationally.

Raphaelle Hanley brought her keen eye, her design skills, and her talent for forging connections between pieces that may appear dissimilar but are united by a shared ethos, in order to form a coherent collection. Atelier Vime is the fruit of this partnership, shaped by the wealth of personal and professional experience that its creators have brought from their "past lives": individual passions for water and the environment, fashion and craftsmanship, photography and images, as well as a shared passion for art, design, furniture, and culture in all its forms. Each of the three members of the studio draws up designs on their own, then they come together around a table to share their ideas and bring them to life.

The principles for each design are always the same: the use of natural materials whose sources can be traced; the conception of objects that will last, can be repaired, and are made by hand by French craftspeople who are experts in their field; the creation of original pieces that are inspired by the history of decorative arts rather than by passing trends.

The furniture and objects in Atelier Vime's collection embody timeless forms inspired by the past that are as varied as the wicker used to create them—this material that is part of our collective unconscious, appearing in an infinite number of incarnations throughout human history.

Whether they are functional or purely decorative, the objects designed by Atelier Vime are imbued with a strong emotional charge; the attention to detail and the perfectly judged proportions make them truly exceptional. Every piece can be made to measure, adapted to suit the needs and preferences of the customer or the space. From a Parisian apartment to a Californian modernist villa, or from an English manor house to a Swiss chalet, Atelier Vime's creations can be found all around the world, as part of minimalist or highly elaborate interiors; they can be incorporated into decors of every style, imparting a sense of humanist serenity and providing the perfect finishing touch.

Atelier Vime's creations are always the result of a collaboration between the creative trio and the craftspeople who fashion the pieces. The dialogue often extends to discussions between the various craftspeople themselves: between the cabinetmaker and the wicker-worker, the metalworker, the woodturner, the brass-worker, the leatherworker, and so on. Whether they are making pieces for Atelier Vime or restoring antiques to be showcased by them, these craftspeople are both the next step in the project and its very heart. Quality does not necessarily mean uniformity, and anyone with a keen eye will certainly find tiny differences between two "identical" objects. They are signs that the pieces are handmade in small series, running counter to the idea of standardization.

The success of the Medici vase—a reinterpretation of a design created by the original studio, Maison Boyer, in the 1940s—has led it to become emblematic of the brand, in its many iterations. However, the studio's products have diversified over time to include numerous different forms, such as mirrors, screens, beds, pelmets, and tableware. And Atelier Vime's range has naturally begun to encompass other materials: ceramics for scented-candle holders or trivets, fabric for tablecloths, metal for canopy beds or reading lamps, and even paper for notebooks. Yet, whatever the object, Atelier Vime is always guided by the same instinct: to bring traditional skills and ancestral materials up to date, not by revolutionizing them but by anchoring them in the present day.

Archived pieces from a set for an Atelier Vime event, at the Lardeur studio in Paris.

DECORATIVE OBJECTS

Medici vase and pedestal

LEFT
On the staircase of an interior combining modernism and tradition, the Medici vase and pedestal perfectly complement the style of interior designer David Netto.

FACING PAGE
The Medici vase on its pedestal, holding a bouquet of flowers, in a maximalist Victorian-inspired library by American interior designer Virginia Tupker.

FACING PAGE
In the home of art and costume historian Clément Trouche in Arles, the Medici sconce has found its place among the discerning collector's eighteenth-century Provençal antiques.

RIGHT
In Paris, beneath a seventeenth-century painting by François Linard, the Medici vase sits alongside an eclectic selection of intriguing and precious objects belonging to artist Emmanuel Pierre.

FACING PAGE
A terra-cotta version of the Medici vase, made using the rope method, stands on a Biedermeier pedestal table. On the wall hangs a portrait in felt-tip pen of Hubert de Givenchy by René Gruau.

Abdel and Alexis

Abdel is a ceramist and head of the clay pottery studio Le Chêne Vert in Anduze, in the Gard département in southern France. Along with artisanal potter Alexis, he worked with Atelier Vime to create a large terra-cotta version of the Medici vase, using the rope method—a traditional technique that is highly complex and fastidious. When the vase is dry, the imprint of the rope that was used as a mold appears on the inside. Abdel and Alexis are among the few craftspeople in France who still practice this technique.

FACING PAGE
The Medici vase reimagined as a trivet in a sunny yellow shade, in the center of a table setting featuring Atelier Vime place mats.

Manon

The young ceramist was chosen by Atelier Vime to create its tableware collection and the glazed terra-cotta Medici trivet/centerpiece. They regularly try out new designs together, such as the glazed terra-cotta colander, which is inspired by their family collection of Provençal tableware.

FACING PAGE
An Atelier Vime scented candle by the edge of the stone basin at the house in Vallabrègues, on a summer's evening.

Gaël

Gaël, a distiller in Provence, is based near Vallabrègues, in a neighboring village. He comes from a family of farmers that goes back three generations. He grows aromatic plants (vervain, lavender, immortelle, lavandin, lemon balm), which he distills to create essential oils and other organic products. Atelier Vime called on him to select the extracts for their scented candles, *eau fraîche* perfumes, and soaps.

The 20s vase

The 20s vase echoes an iconic art deco shape. Marianne Evennou—a French interior designer whose style incorporates elegance, color, and subtlety—chose this vase as the centerpiece for the entrance hall of a Parisian apartment.

Éric

Éric—a rattan-worker whose father cofounded the society of rattan-workers in the 1960s—draws on a rich family history of savoir faire. He is a master of his craft, which consists in creating a wooden template, then softening the rattan by heating it with steam or a blowtorch. The object's final shape is achieved by bending the rattan around the template using a large mallet.

Pelmets

LEFT
The wicker pelmets in an interior by designer David Netto. Here, they bring a touch of warmth to the pared-down space.

FACING PAGE
Extremely versatile, pelmets also work well in more elaborate interiors, such as those by Boston interior designer Nina Farmer, whose work embodies the classic New England style.

Table settings

Combining antique ceramics with those by Atelier Vime, these table settings feature place mats inspired by a traditional braiding stitch, on antique fabric tablecloths.

FACING PAGE
An antique picnic basket is placed open on a nineteenth-century quilted blanket from Médard & Parlier, who were merchants of *indienne* fabrics based in Montpellier. In the background, the pagoda of the Hôtel de Clausonnette, in Beaucaire, can be seen.

Jérôme

Leatherworker Jérôme creates the intricate leatherwork for some of Atelier Vime's most exceptional pieces. Here, in his workshop, he is fashioning the handles for an Atelier Vime picnic basket, which was commissioned by the Mobilier National. Atelier Vime designed this large model for four people; when closed, it can be used as a small table.

LIGHTING

Vallauris ceiling light

In Vallabrègues, the Vallauris ceiling light—inspired by the classic rattan furniture of the postwar French Riviera—disperses a diffuse light over the kitchen table. The Les Vanniers place mats are the result of a collaboration with Marie-Victoire de Bascher.

Facettes ceiling light

A family from Avignon entrusted Atelier Vime with the interior design and decoration of a house from the 1920s. The Facettes ceiling light, with its geometric lines, takes pride of place in this kitchen, which was formerly an artist's studio.

Aramis ceiling light

The Aramis was the first ceiling light designed by Atelier Vime. Based on a handmade metal structure, its complex openwork weave is reflected onto the walls. Here, the model is showcased in an interior by Jake Arnold.

Béatrice

Béatrice, a wicker-worker, has been part of the Atelier Vime team since the studio was founded. She is pictured here at work on the Aramis ceiling light, which takes up to forty hours to weave, depending on the size.

TAMSIN JOHNSON
Irving Penn | CENTENNIAL
CASA MEXICO

Cone ceiling light

FACING PAGE
American interior designer Heidi Caillier creates decors with a refined aesthetic. The Cone ceiling light fits perfectly into this classic, cozy living room.

RIGHT
A cluster of Cone ceiling lights selected by Joséphine Fossey exemplifies the contemporary Provençal style of L'Étoile des Baux luxury vacation home in Baux-de-Provence.

Gabriel ceiling light

The Gabriel ceiling light is the focal point of this large kitchen in Aerin Lauder's family estate in Panama, on the Pacific coast, which was decorated by Daniel Romualdez.

Pascal

Pascal is a cabinetmaker. He works on numerous pieces for Atelier Vime, often making the molds and templates used by the wicker-workers. Here, he is preparing the wood for an oak daybed, which will be partially clad in wicker—a special commission made to order.

LP lamp

LEFT
The LP lamp plays on contrasts in a skillfully designed interior by David Netto.

FACING PAGE
The LP lamp, featuring a hand-painted lampshade by Wayne Pate, enhances the peaceful air of the living room in the home of Clément Trouche, curator at the Musée Provençal du Costume et du Bijou (Provençal Museum of Costume and Jewelry).

Laurent

Metal-worker Laurent creates all of Atelier Vime's metal lamp bases, including the Edith lamp with its complex forms. He is part of the team of loyal craftspeople who have allowed Atelier Vime to grow and create high-quality collections.

Edith lamp

The Edith lamp was the first standing lamp designed by Atelier Vime. It comes in three different sizes, with a large choice of lampshades. An ideal reading lamp, here it provides light for a sofa draped in an Uzbek *suzani* fabric.

FURNITURE

Écailles screen

The Écailles ("Scales") screen, made from natural rattan, wood, and leather, is inspired by art deco motifs and the sea. The creation of this model is a complex and meticulous process.

Leaves cabinet

The Leaves cabinet resulted from the collaboration between three creatives: the artist Wayne Pate designed the floral motif, which was then recreated in hammered metal by brass-worker Matthieu, and rattan-worker Éric created the rattan marquetry around the leaves. On the walls hang photographic works by Erica Lennard and Édouard Boubat, from the Galerie Rouge.

Scalloped daybed

The scalloped shape on this daybed is a classic Atelier Vime touch, which can also be found on a number of different objects and pieces of furniture in the Feston ("Scallop") collection. The motif is inspired by valances: pieces of fabric festooned over the upper part of windows or on canopy beds.

ANTIQUES

Lampshade

A rattan lampshade from the 1940s tops a lamp made of a wooden candelabra in the shape of an eighteenth-century baluster, in Clément Trouche's home in Arles.

Tito Agnoli easy chairs

On the Basque coast, a pair of rattan easy chairs by Tito Agnoli, unearthed by Atelier Vime, fits seamlessly into the joyful, colorful simplicity of Christine Ornano's refined home.

1930s table

In his home on the Brittany coast, Ronan Bouroullec arranges beautiful little bouquets of wildflowers, which he displays in vintage vases on a 1930s rattan and wood table.

Nicolas

Nicolas, a gilder specialized in eighteenth-century artifacts, restores antiques for Atelier Vime. This skilled artisan also creates and restores historical painted decorative features for clients around the world. The art of gilding consists in applying gold leaf or other precious metals to surfaces to embellish or protect them. Gilders use a number of different techniques: gold leaf gilding, water gilding, or mordant gilding.

Fabien

Fabien is just as passionate about restoring an Audoux-Minnet sideboard as a Regency chest of drawers. An essential partner of Atelier Vime's, he, like Nicolas, comes from a Parisian family with a long tradition of craftsmanship.

Daybeds

LEFT
Californian Jake Arnold occasionally leaves Los Angeles to find exceptional pieces to include in his projects. Here, a rare daybed by Louis Sognot is paired with mineral shades in a subdued yet clear-cut color palette.

FACING PAGE
This interior draws on the same color palette, with an Aramis ceiling light suspended above a 1950s daybed, combined with an anthropomorphic vase by Les Dalo and a raffia rug brought back from Spain in the 1950s by Anthony Watson's grandmother.

Walter Sickert

Audoux-Minnet table

This table by Audoux-Minnet, which presides over the room, is a unique piece featuring a hand-painted top by Picard in Vallauris. On the left is Mathieu Matégot's Tropique chair and, on the table, a pair of Fontana lamps by Max Ingrand, designed in 1953. In the center, *La Maternité* by Mathieu Rosianu provides the finishing touch.

Rope lamp

This decor epitomizes the Vime style. It combines rope (the floor lamp and the 1950s Audoux-Minnet coffee table), rattan (the vintage mirror), and wicker (the Atelier Vime sofa). On the wall, *La Petite Reine* by Fernand Léger celebrates the advent of leisure activities inaugurated by the Front Populaire.

Garden furniture

The 1960s modular rattan sofa by Audoux-Minnet evokes relaxation and conviviality in this Provençal project by English interior designer John Tanner.

ARTISTS

Pierre Bergian

Born in Bruges, Belgium, in 1965, Pierre Bergian studied art history and archaeology. This dual passion, along with his interest in architecture, prompted him to create paintings of interiors. His works explore space, light, and structure, and often feature the artistic and ornamental details of rooms bathed in natural light. Among his many projects, which he defines as a meeting between "history, archaeology, and architecture," is his series on the interiors of the Hôtel d'Orruer—Hubert de Givenchy's residence—which was commissioned in 2022 by Christie's.

For Atelier Vime, Pierre Bergian painted the blue bedroom in the house at Vallabrègues. This oil painting, which was reproduced on Atelier Vime's holiday greeting card in 2024, also features on a model in the Le Carnet series, by Atelier Vime.

A drawing of a bedroom in the house at Vallabrègues and a portrait of Anthony Watson, Benoît Rauzy, and Raphaelle Hanley. These watercolor drawings form part of a series that was used to illustrate Atelier Vime's holiday greeting cards for 2021.

Richard Haines

Richard Haines was born in Panama in 1953. After studying art in Virginia, he moved to New York, where he worked for twenty-five years as a designer for fashion houses such as Perry Ellis and Calvin Klein. In 2008, he launched a blog entitled "What I Saw Today," which combines illustrations and humor; it was an instant success. He covers fashion shows for the press, including the *New York Times*, and writes a weekly column for the *Sunday Times*. Miuccia Prada enlisted him to create a series of illustrations based on her Fall/Winter 2012 collection, and Dries Van Noten commissioned him to design fabric prints for the brand's Spring/Summer 2015 collection. Influenced by artists such as Henri de Toulouse-Lautrec and Christian Bérard, Haines's work has brought fashion sketches back into vogue.

Marie-Victoire de Bascher

An artist-on-the-move, whose work lies at the crossroads of design, drawing, and craftsmanship, Marie-Victoire de Bascher founded STUDIO MV in Paris in 2019. In her studio in the Marais district, she cultivates a colorful universe full of humor, populated by a dreamlike bestiary and featuring a natural world that evokes a lost paradise. Marie-Victoire de Bascher has designed motifs for place mats and bespoke tablecloths by Atelier Vime.

The sea provided the inspiration for the Les Coraux motif featured on the cushions around the pool, as well as on the tablecloth adorning this table installed in the courtyard; in the background, a bas-relief by Wayne Pate for Balineum, inspired by the Medici vase, has pride of place.

Forever Picasso

LEFT
This drawing—one of many created for Atelier Vime—represents the studio's creative trio.

FACING PAGE
In the living room of a home in Avignon, a hand-painted lampshade by Wayne Pate adorns a lamp attributed to Jacques Adnet.

Wayne Pate

Furniture, bas-reliefs, murals, lampshades, notebooks—Wayne Pate is adept in all mediums. The New York-based artist, who was born in Texas, assimilates motifs and colors, combining them with a deconstructed geometry. The friendship that connects Wayne Pate to Anthony Watson and Benoît Rauzy nourishes their numerous creative projects together.

Andrea Ferolla

In his lively creations, Italian illustrator Andrea Ferolla depicts a world of sophistication that has caught the eye of fashion and travel magazines, notably *Vogue*, *Yolo Magazine*, and *Airmail Weekly*, which regularly publish his work. Ferolla has also collaborated with a number of luxury brands and iconic hotels, designing large-scale artworks, personalized calligraphy, and emblematic drawings (Rosewood Miramar Beach, Montecito; Le Sirenuse, Positano; Eden Rock – St. Barths; Passalacqua, Lake Como; and Hôtel du Cap-Eden-Roc).

RIGHT
Andrea Ferolla's drawing of a Medici vase and pedestal in a highly fashionable setting includes an affectionate portrait of Raphaelle Hanley.

FACING PAGE
Featuring an illustration by the artist, the silk painted lampshade of the Mare Nostrum lamp is combined with a rattan base by Atelier Vime—the fruit of a collaboration with the brand Chez Dédé in Rome.

Emmanuel Pierre created a holiday greeting card for Atelier Vime, as well as illustrations for notebooks and decorative card boxes. The graphic designer of these items is Virginie Fouin.

Emmanuel Pierre

Specializing in drawing and collage, Emmanuel Pierre was born in 1958 and lives in Paris. After studying at the Beaux-Arts de Paris, he focused on engraving, and the creation of objects and drawings, many of which have been featured in prestigious publications (*The New Yorker*, *The World of Interiors*, *Le Monde d'Hermès*), as well as his iconic children's books. Emmanuel Pierre's unique imagination is exemplified in a wide variety of projects, ranging from the design and creation of Christian Lacroix's Christmas window displays for Galeries Lafayette in 1998 to his garden designs for Atelier Végétal.

ACKNOWLEDGMENTS

This book would not exist without our editors, Julie Rouart, Kate Mascaro, Mélanie Puchault, and Helen Adedotun, and graphic designer Marie-Lou Étienne. To each and every one of you, thank you for your ideas, your keen eye for detail, your patience and positivity, and your expertise.

We would like to express our deepest gratitude to Béatrice Soulard, Éric Pastinelli, Laurent Coloyan, Jean-Marc Blanchard, Daniel Martin, and Pascal Fourrier, for being part of Atelier Vime since our adventure began.

We would also like to acknowledge all of the other craftspeople across France who have joined our team and play an important and passionate role in creating our products.

We are extremely grateful to Lou Amplemont and Yohan Geenen, our invaluable collaborators who design the sets for our events. With Atelier DAR, they bring their essential expertise and experience to Atelier Vime's interior design projects.

We would also like to thank:

Élise Orrier, Pascual Duran, Julien Laprin, Nicolas Delarce, and Fabien Ducret, for the care they take in restoring the houses and objects that we entrust to them.

Marie-Victoire de Bascher, Wayne Pate, Emmanuel Pierre, Richard Haines, Andrea Ferolla, and Pierre Bergian, who are wonderful and inspiring creative partners.

Gaël Davoli for the wicker, the lavender, and the thousand other things that his talents provide us with.

Last but not least, we extend our heartfelt thanks to:

Virginie Fouin, Atelier Vime's graphic designer, for her discerning eye, her skill, and her listening ear.

Patrick and Pierre Frey for their collaboration, and Christine d'Ornano, Marie-Aimée Darblay, Catherine and Anne Lardeur, Aerin Lauder, Marianne Evennou, Joséphine Fossey, Heidi Caillier, Nina Farmer, Clément Trouche, Jake Arnold, David Netto, John Tanner, and Ronan Bouroullec, who very kindly allowed us to use photographs of their homes and their projects around the world to illustrate this book.

Anne Clergue, Francine Deroudille, and Annette Doisneau, for the superb photographs taken by their fathers Lucien Clergue and Robert Doisneau.

Our mothers and our friends for their advice and unfailing support—we owe our freedom and the joy that motivates us to them.

The history of wicker, the basketry craft in Provence, and the village of Vallabrègues that we share on these pages owes a great debt to the wealth of resources in the Bibliothèque Historique de la Ville de Paris, as well as to the expertise of Séverine Guehl-Ines from the Communauté de Communes Beaucaire-Terre d'Argence and the invaluable knowledge of Georges Sudres. We would like to thank them sincerely for their help.

We dedicate this book to Peter, Jacques, Liliane, and Delphine, who will always be with us.

The creative trio that makes up Atelier Vime: Benoît Rauzy, Anthony Watson, and Raphaelle Hanley.

BACK PORTFOLIO CAPTIONS

VII. The staircase in Vallabrègues, lit from above, with corner cupboards that date from the house's original construction.
VIII. The study in Maison Vime, painted in its original colors. On the Beaucaire table by Atelier Vime is a drawing by Jean-Jacques Henner.
IX. A bouquet of flowers arranged by Benoît Rauzy, in a vase by Gio Ponti for Ginori 1735, is placed beside a frame with a detail from a piece of eighteenth-century wallpaper.
X. An eighteenth-century Italian saucer, known as a "trembleuse" (trembler).
XI. The attic at Maison Vime, where antique pieces created by local basket-makers are stored.
XII. A colored version of the Medici vase and pedestal at the Hôtel de Clausonnette, a historic monument in Beaucaire.

PHOTOGRAPHIC CREDITS

© Archives Charmet/Bridgeman Images: p. 19 (right)
© Atelier Lucien Clergue, La Saif 2024: p. 32
© Stefano Bianchetti/Bridgeman Images: p. 22
© Ronan Bouroullec: p. 223
© Bridgeman: pp. 16 (center and right), 17, 20, 21, 31
© Anita Calero/Supervision: p. 212
© Amélie Chassary: pp. 217, 218
© Michael Clifford: pp. 208, 226
© Collection Christian Dior Parfums, Paris: p. 24 (left)
© Robert DOISNEAU/GAMMA RAPHO: p. 33
Photo: Pieter Estersohn © Art Department NY: p. 200
© Tria Giovan: pp. 188, 214
© GrandPalaisRmn (Musée d'Archéologie Nationale)/ Jean-Gilles Berizzi: p. 16 (left)
© Christopher Horwood: pp. 230-231
© Haris Kenjar: p. 210
© KEYSTONE-FRANCE/GAMMA RAPHO: p. 24 (right)
© Ricardo Labougle: p. 189
© P. Locqueneux - Mr. Tripper: p. 211
© Geneviève Lutkin: back portfolio p. VII
© Joanna Maclennan: pp. 48, 50 (right), 51, 53, 54 (left and right), 57, 58, 59 (left), 62 (left and right), 66-67, 68, 74, 75 (left and right), 80, 82 (right), 89, 92-93, 100, 101, 103, 104-105, 106, 108, 109, 120, 121, 126, 127-128, 132, 134-135, 196, 205, 235, back portfolio p. XII
© Marzolino/Shutterstock: p. 30
© Nicolas Mathéus: p. 219
© Nicolas Mathéus and Laurence Dougier: p. 227
© David Mitchell: p. 201
© Yvan Moreau: pp. 35, 138-139, 143, 150, 151, 156 (left and right), 157, 160, 187, 243
© Marie-Pierre Morel: pp. 99, 102 (left and right), 107, 110, 111 (left and right), 116-117, 118, 119, 124 (left and right), 125, 131
Photo © Photo Josse/Bridgeman Images: p. 23
© Private collection: pp. 24 (center), 25, 28, 29, 36, 37
© Matthieu Salvaing: p. 222
© SOAS/Bridgeman Images: p. 19 (left)
Photo: Tarker/Bridgeman Images: p. 18
© Grégory Timsit: p. 198
© Théophile Trossat: p. 7
© Jean-Pierre Vaillancourt: pp. 229, 236
© Anthony Watson: front cover, front portfolio pp. I, II, III, IV, V, VI, pp. 4, 8, 11, 12-13, 14, 26, 38, 40, 43, 45, 46, 47, 49, 50 (left), 52, 55, 56, 59 (right), 60, 61, 63, 64, 65, 69, 70, 71 (left and right), 72, 73, 76, 77, 78, 81, 82 (left), 83, 84 (left and right), 85, 86, 87, 90 (left and right), 91, 95, 96, 97, 113, 114, 115, 122, 123, 130, 137, 141, 142 (left and right), 144, 145, 146-147, 148, 149, 152, 153 (left and right), 154 (left and right), 155, 158, 159, 161, 162, 163, 165, 166-167, 168, 169, 170, 171, 172 (left and right), 173, 174, 175, 176-177, 178-179, 180-181, 182, 183, 184, 190, 191, 192, 193, 194, 195, 197, 199, 202, 203, 204, 206, 207, 209, 213, 215, 216, 220, 221, 224, 225, 228, 232, 233, 234, 237, 238, 239, 240, 241, back portfolio pp. VIII, IX, X, XI

ARTISTS' COPYRIGHTS

INTERIORS